D1144993

MOVING WITH THE TIMES

Valerie Preston-Dunlop

MOVING WITH THE TIMES

Valerie Preston-Dunlop

THE NOVERRE PRESS

First published in 2017
by The Noverre Press, a division of Dance Books Ltd.,
Southwold House, Isington Road, Binsted, Hampshire GU34 4PH

ISBN 978-1-906830-80-9

Cover photographs:
Paolo Tosi and Roland Watkins, Laban Collection.

Contents

Acknowledgements

Without helpful archivists I could not have included so many images. So grateful thanks to Jane Fowler for allowing me to include material from the Laban Collection and for dealing with my frustrations on copyright issues. Also to the patience of Michael Reed of the English National Ballet Archive, and the efficiency of the Bern Canton Archive, the Harvard Theatre Collection, the Ruhr Museum Archive and the National Resource Centre for Dance.

Kitty Watkins, Sally Archbutt and Charles Fox have allowed me to include images from their private collections as have members of my family. The following photographers have collaborated generously Peter Sayers, Nigel Voak, Toni Nandi, Paolo Tosi, Kyle Stevenson and Pau Ros.

I am ever grateful for the technical expertise of Ian Peppiat and Richard Pickvance who can retrieve, enhance, rescue, upgrade and trim to turn a hope into a usable image.

With regard to the text, especial thanks to Roger Dunlop and Emma Preston-Dunlop for not forbidding me from writing about their childhood.

Rona Sande deserves the highest accolade for having listened to every slice of my story as it emerged and keeping me on the narrow path between what one might say and what one should say.

Lastly my thanks to David Leonard who agreed enthusiastically to publish this book and to his expert editor Liz Morrell for making a book out of text and image and fielding my last-minute second thoughts.

CHAPTER 1

1930

Nursery Life

Here for me is South London, Blackheath to be precise, a suburb that refuses to stop being a village. Being born in these parts I have come home to roost to enjoy my last occupations coloured by familiarity.

A few weeks ago I drove past the house where I was born en route for a celebratory meal with my nearest and dearest, Roger my son, with his wife and family, and my daughter Emma. My story begins in 1930 at the Vicarage of St Mary's Lewisham where my father, Arthur Llewellyn Preston, known as Bill, was the incumbent. He loved being the father of his flock and was loved in return.

The handsome Queen Anne house stands at the T junction of Lewisham High Street and Ladywell Road. Currently occupied by the National Health Service, it has inevitably changed internally but the garden is as it was in my childhood without the swing on the tree and the trams rumbling past. Having achieved three daughters, Robina, Alison and Elizabeth, my mother, Nancy, being forty, had agreed to a fourth pregnancy in a last gasp attempt to produce a son. The first words said to me by my sisters, so the story goes, was 'We don't really want you but you are rather sweet,' a bit of a mixed welcome. With hindsight I can see my gender was a disappointment to my father and I was to prove a challenge to my loving but not-so-young mother.

Life at Lewisham was very different from the average vicarage today. St Mary's was a well-endowed living, in the main the populace went to church. Bill and his friend Dr Nockolds, director of Lewisham's large hospital, were two prominent establishment figures in the town.

Our household boasted a cook, butler, two nursemaids, gardener-handyman, kitchen maid and daily cleaners. Bill had six curates and they were regulars at the vicarage. All in all Nancy had quite a domain to oversee and a new arrival, me, a girl to boot, was, I suspect, a bit much.

Before I was three we moved to Blackheath, Bill being promoted to Bishop of Woolwich, Suffragan to the Bishop of Southwark, with Southwark Cathedral by London Bridge his place of worship. All I knew was that the man who wore gaiters, a frock, and a purple shirt, had a study and smoked a pipe, was my father whom I hardly ever saw. The other person I saw occasionally was, I learnt, my mother. My constant companion and love of my life was Nanny, Miss Hilda Barton, with whom I shared the nursery on the first floor. There I had breakfast, lunch and tea, played and learned. The night nursery, up the next flight of stairs, I shared with Elizabeth, three years my senior, and of course, Nanny.

By the time I reached four I was allowed down to the dining room for Sunday lunch, just for the pudding course, where Nanny abandoned me to the grown ups. It felt special and I was on my best behaviour, as taught by Nanny. After lunch we all gathered in the drawing room. My first embroidery, six inches square, was painstakingly stitched in that room and an effort it was to complete, Sunday after Sunday. Nancy sang and played ballads at the grand piano while Bill supervised my sisters roasting chestnuts in the open fire. I have embroidered dozens of cushions and chair seats in my time and they adorn my Blackheath living room but this little square was the start of it. I have just completed one for Ralph, my latest great-great-nephew. With numbers and letters round a Noah's Ark I think he will like it.

I must have been six when I accompanied my father to the nursing home next door to learn how to talk to old ladies and gentlemen in bed, my first experience of concern for people less fortunate than myself. I understood that visiting the sick was the expected norm for people born into our kind of 'station in life'. Looking back I cringe at the accepted stratification of society in those days and our family was a prime example of a paternalistic model with my mother and father instilling in us girls that we were privileged and thereby had a duty to care for any and all who were not so lucky.

The kitchen in the basement of our house was a forbidden place where we children only descended on Nanny's afternoon off. There Dobby, Edith Dobbins, the cook, who was to remain with us all her days, ruled her below-stairs household and entertained 'the tradesmen' to morning tea and beef dripping bread as she gave her orders for meat, fish, groceries, vegetables for delivery the same afternoon. Her constant companion was

Polly the parrot who had learned regrettable language from Robert the butler, ate peanuts in their shell and was not fond of little girls as the scar on my thumb records to this day.

Blackheath still resonates time past. The toyshop, the pond, the dentist's surgery were there in the 1930s. On the heath Greenwich Park is where Nanny pushed me daily, she in uniform, I in velvet-collared coat and buttoned-up gaiters, to meet up with other nannies and their charges by the duck pond. I drive now, parking in a Disabled bay, give peanuts to the squirrels and watch young mothers with their mobile phones and, at weekends, office workers en masse with their trainer somewhat desperately keeping fit with aerobic routines.

The large houses in Vanburgh Terrace, now turned into flats, were where my sisters and I went to tea with other little girls. The letterbox in the wall of St John's Park is still there where I posted my carefully drawn pictures for Mr Ivel, an out-of-work miner from County Durham. For some reason it was thought caring and loving for children of our station in life to 'adopt' a distressed person in the Depression, the financial slump after the 1929 Wall Street crash with its flood of unemployment. I believe my parents contributed financially to him and my drawings were their way of introducing me to the future responsibilities of our 'class'.

The horror with which I write that word now, as a Quaker, is profound, where equality of all people is a basic tenet. My life has ricocheted between privilege and hardship, patrimony and socialism, but those early beginnings linger, sometimes in my voice, sometimes in my ease of talking to all and everyone whether the Duke of Kent, Trinity Laban's patron, or Kevin, the homeless man who sits outside Shepherds grocery by day and sleeps beneath the Quaker Meeting House canopy by night.

A block of flats now stands in place of Woolwich House, No 22, St John's Park, the abode of the Bishop of Woolwich, just round the corner from the heath where the circus and funfair still stake their patch on bank holiday weekends as they always have.

The Royal Naval College down Maze Hill in Greenwich is no longer where teenage ratings learn their marine trade but is the campus of the new multicultural Greenwich University and of Trinity Laban College of Music. Being an Honorary Fellow of the Trinity Laban Faculty of Music, I hear aspiring pianists, trumpeters, guitarists filling King Charles Court in place of the astronomy, map-reading, lanyard and knot making of naval cadets. The famous Painted Hall is now visited by tourists who crane their necks to wonder at the ceiling. My sisters and I attended formal Christmas tea parties there, given by the Naval College Admiral, Officers and Ratings, Nanny standing behind our chairs. After tea the excitement began as we explored a secret grotto, or confronted a pirate. The test of bravery was coming home with a skull and crossbones printed on your arm. Elizabeth and Alison always achieved it but I was too scared.

My dame school, run by Miss Adams, was demolished for the A2 motorway but the identical next-door houses are still there, unchanged, on Shooters Hill Road. I pass them in the 89 bus on my way to Thompson's Nurseries where I buy the essentials for my pride-and-joy vegetable patch and food for the birds to whom I give as much love as I gave my children. Miss Adams' school was where I first danced under the penetrative eye of portly Miss Moore. Little did she or I know that her beautiful teaching of the waltz would be the beginning of my life-long career, the transformation from curly-haired plump five year old to silver-haired Dr Valerie Preston-Dunlop, Laban Dip, Adv Dip Ed, MA dist, PhD, Hon. FTL.

Miss Moore taught the old-fashioned Molly and Mary method, Molly for your left foot, Mary for your right. One Wednesday afternoon instead of waltzing in a square, forward side together, back side together, we advanced down the room, forward side together, *forward* side together and for the first time in my life my little body felt the thrill of motion, the heavenly flow of moving through space. I left the school hall and entered the cosmos. That was eighty years ago and feels like today.

The imposing Blackheath Halls, where Trinity Laban College of Music students play lunchtime jazz, I knew as the venue for the children's Christmas pantomime. Last season I sang there, being a somewhat rusty alto in the Blackheath Choir giving my all to Brahms German Requiem and loving it. I must have music in my life. If I can no longer dance then I will sing.

This morning Tony fixed my silvered hair in the salon on Tranquil Vale. It had to be today because this afternoon Henrik, the Danish filmmaker, will bring his camera crew to Trinity Laban to shoot a sequence for a documentary on Monte Verita 1913. I will ad lib to camera on the dance pioneer Rudolf Laban as I have done so often, this time on his School for the Arts at Monte Verita, the Mountain of Truth, the idyll of experimental alternative living a century ago in the Swiss Ticino. The salon used to house the furniture show room of Hinds department store where my mother bought all the things needed for our house. Where now the village is polluted by constant traffic, in my childhood horses and carts and bicycles were the norm with a few very new Ford cars, and we had one.

Our family at that time consisted of Robina, thirteen years my senior who I discovered years later was my half-sister, her father being Captain Francis Ward, killed in the First World War, in the morass of mud at Passchendaele. Robina was remote to me, an elegant teenaged redhead, a budding actress at the Royal Academy of Dramatic Art, definitely not helping with child-care.

For quite a while Elizabeth, known as Lindy, who was three years my senior, shared my nursery life. She went off to Miss Adams in the morning leaving me with Nanny but returned for bread and butter, scone and cake for tea. Lindy was my first playmate, a compliant girl with long plaits, already a budding pianist beyond her years. She re-appears as important to me throughout my story. Alison was six years older than me and I hardly remember her at all at that time. She regarded Elizabeth and I as the Littles with whom she had as little to do as possible.

She was twelve, the oldest of the Preston girls and big enough to feel she should compete with her redhead half-sister Robina. She did it by being academically studious, which Robina was not, and mature enough to fit in with the grown-ups which we Littles were not. Of course we did do things all together as sisters, especially playing with Rosemary and Geoffrey, Dr Nockolds' children, he being the superintendent of Lewisham Hospital. Rosemary, now in her nineties, will stay a night with me this week en route to a funeral. How often funerals occur these days. She had a career in the Foreign Office and an OBE for her efforts. We will share a bottle of good wine, talk politics and world affairs.

Under Lewisham hospital lay a labyrinth of passageways for the heating system, drains and laundry, all things that children should not get involved in. But we did or rather the older ones did and I was dragged along, a nuisance who could not keep up. We got there through a 'secret passage', alias a cupboard, near a ward by the stairs to the basement. We nipped in when the nurses were not looking. Our friend, a porter, kept watch and whistled when the coast was clear.

I recall one regrettable day when we got it badly wrong. For some reason Geoffrey, aged eleven, commanded that Elizabeth should try a new entry. We complied, Geoffrey being, to me, wicked and adventurous. But the lattice gate to this other staircase was locked.

Geoffrey, being a sporty boy, climbed over. Elizabeth, encumbered by me, was in a dilemma when the strident footfall of Dr Nockolds could be heard echoing down the corridor definitely heading in our direction. I was popped into a huge wicker laundry basket on pain of death to keep quiet, while Elizabeth who was Dr Nocky's beloved goddaughter prepared to charm him into 'helping her find her way home'. Of course Dr Nocky, being the superintendent, had the key to the gate and down he went to return with Geoffrey held by his ear, Alison and Rosemary penitent behind. Off they all went leaving me marooned in a smelly laundry basket. I must have been rescued but how remains a faded memory.

Recently I wrote a letter to my MP on 'Save Lewisham Hospital'. The powers that be have threatened to close the Accident & Emergency department with financial savings their key thought. On many occasions I have sat patiently for triage having broken my arm, cracked my ankle, I have sat with my husband John after he broke his hip, rushed in as my friend Dorothy suffered a heart attack. Closing the A&E is more than a change of medical care. It would be the end of an era for me. We will see what Heidi Alexander MP can achieve.

Alison and Rosemary, alias Bloody Jo and Bloody Jim, were the joint captains of our pirate gang. They dressed the part with skull and crossbones and scarlet kerchieves. Brandishing cutlasses they forced me to walk the plank over the garden pond. Nanny rescued me and that is why I loved her so much. When Rosemary went to boarding school, being the oldest, she wrote a letter to 'Bloody Jo, Bishops House, Blackheath'. The postman was shocked at 'swear words to a house of religion' so our father thought it best to ban the correspondence.

Some Sundays we would walk across Blackheath to St Margaret's Church (a long way for little legs) for morning service, always a bit of a trial for a five year old. I could sing with the congregation, I could kneel with my head just below the parapet and play quietly with a permitted toy. The lessons read out by a serious man I could sometimes follow, for the stories in the Old Testament, David and Goliath, Isaac and Jacob et al were quite exciting and my childish mind listened for the expected gory bits. It was the sermon that was the problem but my resourceful mother was on to it. She took my plump hand firmly in her elegant one and with her middle finger traced patterns on my palm, slowly and continuously for maybe twenty minutes. An exquisite calm came over me as I anticipated where her finger would move next.

Polly, my granddaughter, has just returned to Chichester University for her third year reading music as a trumpeter. I saw her there in the pit for Gilbert and Sullivan's *Gondoliers*. When I visit Polly again I will drive on a few miles south to Selsey on Sea, for that is where in the 1930s we spent our family holidays in one of the fashionable railway carriage bungalows on the cliff. They have all fallen into the sea by now but then it was idyllic, the only time we all met as a family. Bill drove us down in the Ford 10 via Guildford and The Hogs Back. Once on Selsey's cliff path we children took it in turns to stand on the running board and poke our heads out of the open roof.

While our parents disappeared to sail at Itchenor, Robina took off in an open-topped car with a boy friend, Alison remained stuck in a book while we younger girls, with Nanny, took to the beach, the lovely sandy castle-worthy beach. We caught shrimps for tea and paddled, Nanny bringing towels and ginger biscuits to warm us up.

What did I take away from this strange but idyllic nursery life? Good manners, kindliness, respect for all, how to play, how to share. It was a silver spoon childhood, one that prepared me for a life that was to disappear dramatically through an event that left me sprawling.

Above My father and sisters: 'We don't really want you but you are rather sweet'

Above right My sister Elizabeth

Below My mother Nancy with her four girls, Robina, Elizabeth, me and Alison

With my sister Elizabeth making sand castles on Selsey beach

Nanny, Miss Hilda Barton, at my wedding

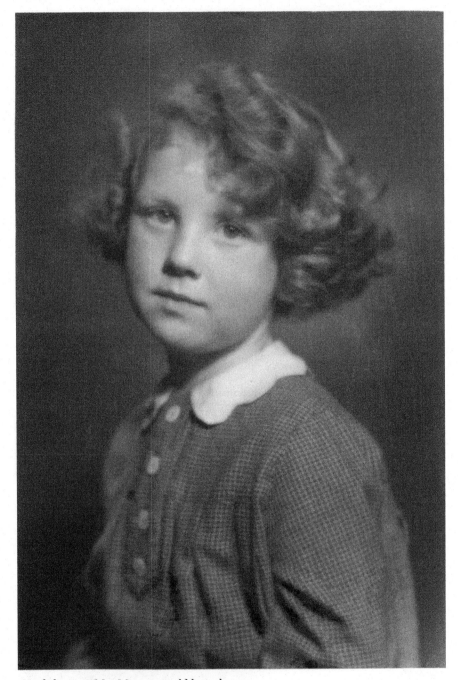

Aged three as Mrs Moore would have known me

CHAPTER 2
1936
All Change

By now in my life I have encountered death again and again but 1936 was the first, unexpected, a catastrophe for the family. My father, aged fifty-two, died of a heart attack on holiday aboard his brother's yacht Lorna, sailing in the Baltic Sea. Wham, just like that, from brimming with life and endeavour, he went, the end of a life full of promise, the end of a dream for my mother, and for me an end to a silver-spoon life. Instead confusion, upheaval, loss of everything I knew that made me safe. I was six years old with no skills whatever for independent living and yet that was what I was to face.

Bill's funeral I have described in all its pomp and miserable detail in my book on my mother's life, *Nancy's Story*. In reality it was a non-event for me. I was sent away while the tragic happenings unfolded. My trauma was the stark loss not of a father whom I hardly knew but of Nanny, my friend, my mentor, my anchor. My mother was left with no husband, no income, no home and four girls to bring up alone. It seems outrageous now but bishop's widows received no pension. The church was stuck in a time when bishops of yore were the youngest sons of moneyed landed gentry. My father was the youngest son but not of landed gentry.

So we moved with one devastating blow from relative opulence to decisive penury, dependent on the generosity of Bill's brothers. They found us a house in a village in Bill's diocese, Limpsfield in Surrey, and paid its mortgage while my mother set about using her skills as a seamstress to earn enough to feed her family, for all she had was her miniscule WW1 widow's pension. Dobby, the cook, and Timmins, the gardener, a disabled ex-miner, came with us, both with board and lodging but no pay. That arrangement could only have been acceptable in a time of dire unemployment for where else might they go in the Depression of the 1930s? Dobby had been with my mother since Frank's appalling death at Passchendaele so she felt herself part of the family.

To help her recover from the onslaught of Bill's death Nancy was taken for a six-week retreat by wealthier friends during which I, and Elizabeth, went to board temporarily at The Manor House, our new school. While that might not seem a big issue, for Elizabeth it was quite exciting, for me it was an event that led to all sorts of lasting difficulties. I had never tied my own shoelaces, or brushed my hair, I couldn't read properly for Nanny read to me, or make my bed. Nanny had done everything, so in this new circumstance I failed on every front, was late, with the wrong book, dishevelled and probably demanding. I was considered naughty and difficult and that stuck in the sense that for a short time I came to believe it myself. Nanny's 'There's a good girl' was a long way from failure after failure.

The Manor House School is no more. In its place is a posse of bijou residences where once were classrooms, a netball pitch and a swimming pool. Of course I survived my early childhood trauma there but it left a legacy for I discovered before long that I was neither naughty nor stupid. With a determination to pay no attention to obstacles or to listen to opinions I decided by seven years old to plough my own furrow and that I have done.

The Manor House experience was basically catastrophic. To help my mother we were allowed to stay at school till 7pm, with the boarders. Nine in the morning to seven in the evening is a long day for a six year old. Being the youngest in the school by a year and emotionally at sea, but no fool, and clearly opinionated, I struggled. After tea we all sat in the dining hall and did homework, or they did, but since I could barely read those two hours were a daily nightmare.

Timmins came to walk us home, and Dobby gave us supper so I still hardly saw my mother. Whatever problems I was having, and there were many, I had to solve myself. Solace came in the form of Miss Nicholson, a visiting ballet teacher. Wednesday became the focus of my week and indeed the focus of my life. As my hand touched the ballet barre in the school hall I entered heaven as my clumsy little body learnt to swoop and swirl and my feet to *pas de basque, assemblé, changement*.

But I learnt another lesson that stayed with me for Miss Nicholson, superb teacher that she was, had a favourite, Mary, a pretty girl, a talented dancer, on whom Nicholson doted and of whose future success she dreamed. But Mary grew, she was clearly going to be tall, too tall for ballet. Nicholson dropped her, abandoned her, paid no more attention to her. I watched this, and observed what thwarted adult ambition could do. I learnt not only what ballet can offer but also that it can ruin. Even aged eight I was aware of the tragedy of Mary's downfall and my childish sense of fairness was outraged. I continued dancing, it was too precious to lose, but I vowed I would never look Nicholson in the eye again, and I didn't.

With my sisters, I was a proud bridesmaid at Robina's summer wedding, paid for by her father's well-off family, because try as she might, Nancy could not afford it. Then all change. Sunday September the 3rd, 1939, being the fateful day when England declared war on Germany, I found myself and Elizabeth whisked away to Somerset with Dobbie as our carer. So began life as an evacuee in the home of my reluctant godmother, she being one of the generation of unmarried women after WW1. We attended a local religious school and had to change our clothes to enter the chapel, it being obligatory to wear a white novice's veil and a St Catherine's tunic. I sent a weekly note to my mother, one of which sums up my feelings. 'We go to chapple twice a day. I have to ware a fowl vale.'

I was nine rising ten, bolshie and seriously unable to spell. Worse, little girls who did not know their Our Father and General Thanksgiving were penalised by being the only ones to carry a prayer book into chapel, for all to see. I could say both but to qualify one had to recite them alone to the headmistress. Pig headed as I was I regarded that as an affront to my heritage as a bishop's daughter and would not, so ended up as the only one in my class with the dreaded prayer book. And of course I never had the veil, the tunic and the prayer book together in the right place at the right time.

The school was hopelessly overcrowded with unwelcome evacuees. My classroom was makeshift in a stable. As the autumn turned to winter it was freezing, my fingers and toes were covered in chilblains. One day, to get out of the cold, an adder slid through the window and that did it. I became quite ill with the trauma of it all and developed a rash and a fever. The godmother's aged mother declared she 'would not have sickness brought to the house' so we returned home, to Limpsfield, just in time for the Dunkirk crisis and the drama in the sky overhead of the Battle of Britain.

Each day the German planes flew over with the intention of eliminating the RAF and incapacitating their airfields and hastily made airstrips of which there were many nearby, Biggin Hill, Croydon, Kenley, Detling, West Malling. We were on the direct approach to London that the enemy had to dominate if they were to invade successfully, as was expected. We children only half understood the critical nature of the battle above. It was exciting to watch the Spitfires and Hurricanes harass the invaders, with incredible aerial manoeuvres, sputtering gunfire, whining as planes dived and delved and shrill screeching as one fell in flames. It was almost fun to hide under the bracken as a Messerschmitt dived in your direction.

Everywhere houses were prepared for bombing. We had sandbags piled up in the porch covering the front door, all windows pasted with sticky tape against flying glass, buckets of sand ready for incendiary bombs all over the house. Many families dug an air-raid shelter in the garden, ours was an indoor strengthened corridor. As the Battle of Britain ended, the Blitz on London began. You slept with your siren suit, what we would call a 'onesie' today, ready on your bed with your gas mask and emergency suitcase next to it. When the Air Raid Siren wailed, you gathered everything, ran to the shelter and dossed down crammed like sardines, all of us, plus the people evacuated from London billeted on us. And this happened nightly for eight months, one week and two days as Hitler determined to bomb London to smithereens.

With the strictest curfew and blackout in force we only used torches. You listened for particular sounds, the wumph wumph wumph of the heavy bombers, flying over in their hundreds, the shrill whine of a falling bomb, the ack ack ack of the guns, the whistle of the local Air Raid Warden. Everyone was on alert for incendiaries, the silent firebombs, so from time to time an adult crept out to check the attic, or peep through the blackout. One night was the worst, the firebombing of the London docks. We could see a red glow twenty miles away visible over the North Downs, a ghastly halo over London. The bombs that fell on our bit of Surrey came as the Luftwaffe returned home, dumping on us what they had failed to drop on target. Then the All Clear sounded and you slept as best you could.

The cold was the worst part of rationing. To save fuel a household was permitted to use one electric fire only. So huddle we did, all of us round the one bar in Dobbie's bed-sitting room while knitting khaki socks for soldiers and waterproof gloves for sailors. The dining room was given over to a bombed out London couple, a traumatised retired nurse had the spare room, six Canadian soldiers occupied the attic, an unmarried mother and child slept somewhere, two evacuee five year olds shared my bedroom, and on occasion New Zealand airmen on forty-eight hour leave joined us. We almost ran out of food once. Nancy announced that the only thing left was potatoes, so potato balls we ate, flavoured with herbs from the garden and I recall, meagre as they were, they tasted delicious.

It was deemed unwise for me to return to the Manor House School so I was bussed to another one and enjoyed the best year of primary schooling ever. At last a teacher got to grips with my talents and my shortcomings, a recognition of my prowess in maths and science making all the difference. I could succeed and succeed I did. But it was not to last for at twelve years old I had to move on, back to the Manor House.

By now many children had left, evacuated, so the school was struggling. I was again the youngest in my class of ten girls, the oldest being sixteen. The headmistress was a literature and history scholar, my weakest subjects, for which I never achieved more than four out of ten. I recall one holiday homework: 'Write a One Act Play.' You must be joking! I did not even know what a one act play was. For one history homework we were to write on the American War of Independence. What? America? Is that war happening now? We did do sums which I could do standing on my head but no science as the lab was occupied by soldiers. I was lost again, angry, and I cut up rough, so rough that it was suggested to my poor mother that she find a larger school to cater for my unruly needs.

So at thirteen I was packed off to boarding school.

My father, Arthur Preston, on board *Lorna* the morning he died

Above Nicholson's *London Cries*, me central, Elizabeth right

Left Ballet with Miss Nicholson, Mary with Elizabeth

Leading the bridesmaids at Robina's wedding to John Wyldbore-Smith,
Elizabeth behind me

CHAPTER 3

1944

A Chequered Education

Today I am on a train to Newbury to be picked up at the station by Roger's wife Venetia for a happy day or two's stay in their converted farmhouse. Roger may be in Prague, or Dublin or Atlanta, one never knows but he will fly in and join us as and when business allows, to enjoy a family weekend, maybe with his children Polly and Jack too.

Being a grandmother is an interesting experience that I resisted in principle since my own grandmother, Nancy's dreaded stepmother, was a horror of the first order, in looks, behaviour and child-baiting. Since grannyhood in my mind was associated with all things suspect and aged one contemptibly, I was not into it. So I am known as Milly, actually short for mother-in-law, and that means I can enjoy being part of a multigenerational happening without ever registering that I am in fact an elderly grandmother.

As Polly and Jack grew they came to my bedroom in the morning where I had cunningly, I thought, hidden sweeties or some such luscious thing which they found and enjoyed, then shifted gear, sat on the bed, to play a cut and thrust game of cards, Beggar My Neighbour or Auntie Betty's Rummy, or Snap, with no holds barred. So I was both spoily Milly and on-the-level playmate and that is how it has stayed.

Newbury station, on the other hand, is fraught with feelings of despond for, aged thirteen, and having been removed from the Manor House School, I found myself entrained for boarding school, Downe House to be precise. It appeared to me to be in the middle of nowhere. Paddington Station has forever been blighted by the horrors of 'the school train', the hour-long transition from the embrace of family to isolation.

Being a boarder in war-time meant abandonment for three months at a time since no one could travel, no one could visit, or telephone, so different from life with a mobile phone, Facebook and Twitter. Once again I was the youngest in my class and joining in January, the wrong time of the school year. All the other girls had formed friendships. My skills at ploughing my own path held me together but marked me as a bit of a loner.

But, wonder of wonders, this enlightened school taught creative dance to every girl, from eleven to eighteen. Mary Baron, to me a beautiful redhead sent from heaven, was my saviour. I fell in love with her in my schoolgirl way, and my one hour per week of dancing bliss made the rest diminish to nothing. My first experience of 'a movement choir', *The Snow Queen*, took place at Downe. Every class in the school had a role to play, a scene to dance, as a flowing river, as a storm of snow, as the Queen's dancing courtiers... My tiny solo part as the heroine's mother sealed my career path.

It was pure luck that my mother knew of Olive Willis, the headmistress. Olive was one of the thousands of unmarried women in post-WW1 England, but she was totally contrary to what one thought of as a spinster. She was sixty but 'with it', in the jargon, and ahead of every prank or lie a scheming teenage girl might present. She was large, unmoveable, with two enormous dogs for company. I admired her forthwith as a fellow traveller different from any teacher I had met so far.

It being 1944 all schools had the greatest difficulty in finding staff. Any woman of useful age had been called up for war service in the ATS or the WAAFS or the WRENS or the VADs so Downe's teachers were a mishmash of exempted women cajoling a hundred and eighty girls many of whom, like me, had had a chequered school career, evacuated from one safe haven to another, and an unsettled home life with fathers in the forces and parents separated. In any event I survived a somewhat troubleful three years where my academic success was countered by unsettled behaviour.

Rules abounded, some associated with rationing, especially sweets where each girl had her box with her weekly allowance, doled out during the after-Sunday-lunch rest. One Mars Bar had to last a month so each bite was a savoured ritual. Elizabeth, beloved sister, sent me a Cadbury bar from her rations, in the post. The parcel had to be opened under scrutiny and I was instructed to return it since it was deemed unfair for one girl to have more sweets than others. Return it? You are joking.

So began my first illicit scheming, egged on by two form mates (beneficiaries). We unpacked the wrapping, divided the bar into three, one bit each, and hid them. We collected mud from the lacrosse pitch, formed it into the likeness of the bar, parceled it up and I presented it to the house mistress for posting back to Elizabeth, my face the epitome of innocence. Did she guess? Probably, for mud is heavier than chocolate.

My classmates were well on in study of the curriculum for School Certificate so it was thought impossible for me to join their lessons in science mid-stream. Instead I was put into a set of other girls to study German. Little did I realise how useful that would prove for my later sojourn in Essen. The teacher was the most unattractive woman I had ever met, with greasy black hair tucked into a grubby band round her head. Notwithstanding, I found the language interesting and played a game with myself to definitely be the best in the class in *gesprockener Deutsch* so if I ever met a fugitive German I would know how to defend myself: *Hände Hoch!*

She also taught Latin, obligatory for all, where *Caesar's Gallic Wars* were the text. That proved more than my patience could tolerate for how many times can one become interested in an army striking camp? I fear I was not easy to teach and I failed and that mattered in those days because to gain entry to university you must pass with credit in Latin. Ah well.

The uneven level of teaching was exposed by the School Certificate Art examination for which we had had no preparation whatever. While we painted and drew with the best we had had no study of artists per se. Faced with a written paper on the History of Art I chose a Holbein cartoon to discuss. Who was Holbein? What was a cartoon if not the jokes in the *Daily Mail?* I learned a very useful but amoral lesson as by careful scrutiny of the illustration I fooled the examiner that I knew what Holbein did and was myself a budding art critic for I not only passed but did so with high marks. Not a good lesson to learn.

Eventually sciences came my way. I discovered the magic of the blue of copper sulphate, the gills of a stinking dog fish, osmosis, Bunsen burner, pipette, test tubes... This seemed a more satisfactory way of looking at the world than the transubstantiation taught in Chapel in my preparation for confirmation or the virgin birth of Jesus Christ. What? Really?

Somewhat to the confusion of my housemistress I knew a good deal about sex. Being the youngest of four girls I could hardly avoid it. It was discovered that I coped with my period by using a tampon, instructed by Alison. Alarmed, Miss X took me aside to make sure I did not pass on this skill to any other girl since some mothers would disapprove or not even know how to use one. Such was the ignorance abounding in female sex education.

Two events in my final year at Downe had lasting effects. A new inexperienced gym teacher invited us to leap over a horse using a new springboard. Being the first in line I bounded on to the board, rose into the air and missing the horse altogether landed in a heap on the gymnasium floor doing serious damage to a knee. Surgery followed with foreboding that I would not be dancing for some time, if at all. The idea that I would miss my hour in Mary Baron's company was alarming because indeed she was throughout my time at Downe the only person that mattered. Dance Club on Monday evenings was the zenith of heaven.

I did recover, but slowly, and to compensate was given the lead role of Bluntschli, a mercenary soldier, in Bernard Shaw's *Arms and the Man*. At some point Bluntschli, hidden, climbs secretly onto a balcony and appears, slowly, through heavy curtaining, amid titillating tension. The gasps from the Upper Fourths were gratifying. I discovered the thrill of performing, counter-balancing that pleasure with the effort of calculus, statics and dynamics, the history of ideas and the sexual proclivity of the mollusc.

Then catastrophe loomed. Trusted Olive Willis was to retire, coinciding with my falling out with the woman destined to take over the headship. We were not permitted to keep money but I did have a Postal Order for 5/- hidden under my mattress. I needed to be able to get home, that much autonomy I was not prepared to forfeit. Naively, I thought that a Postal Order might get me there. Said woman found it and hauled me up for a 'jaw', alias a talking to. My reply: 'What were you doing sneaking under my mattress?' and I demanded a discussion with Olive Willis. In the end she never did take over the headship so perhaps I did the school a service. Then Mary Baron was to leave. Void, chasm, emotional trauma. I told my mother I must leave Downe. I was sixteen.

At that very point Rudolf Laban opened the Art of Movement Studio in Manchester and Mary Baron suggested to my mother that I go there to train as a dancer. My somewhat desperate mother, despairing with what to do with this troublesome girl, found the suggestion a godsend. So completely ill-equipped to face the world by myself but focused and ready to move on, with neither my mother nor myself having any idea what I was going to, I left school and embarked on an extraordinary adventure.

'Milly' with Polly and Jack

Cast as the mother of the heroine in *The Snow Queen*

One corner of the movement choir *The Snow Queen* at Downe House

Venetia Dunlop, Roger's wife, at their home in Berkshire

CHAPTER 4

1947

The Art of Movement Studio

I am walking along Millbank from the Houses of Parliament to Tate Britain invited to speak at a celebration of Kurt Schwitters and his Merzbarn heritage. I encountered Schwitters' barn some sixty plus years ago, in 1948 as a scrawny student, an ignorant but fearless teenager and that is what I will talk about. But how did that happen?

As cultural life in Europe reignited after WW2, two remarkable men embraced, the German Dada artist Kurt Schwitters and the Hungarian dance giant Rudolf Laban, both exiles, refugees, penniless and suffering the physical and mental scars of Nazism. A war-damaged office in Oxford Road, Manchester, was the place, a bare room, turned into the practice space of the Art of Movement Studio. It was to become my workplace for nigh on four years for the sweat and effort that a dancer's training is.

Schwitters and Laban had met briefly once before, mid WW1, in neutral Zurich, with the Cabaret Voltaire in its full anarchic flood led by the self-named Dadaists Tristan Tzara and Hugo Ball. Nightly they stunned and affronted Swiss audiences by their outrageous offerings, harangued by poetry thrown at them in three languages simultaneously, recited backwards, interrupted, while crouched under a grand piano, delivered muffled under a waste paper basket, standing on one leg on a chair, or any other *mise en scene* that might break the respectable recitation mode of art salons. While the young men of Europe slaughtered each other in bestial and tragic war Laban's dancers partook in the mayhem, improvising on the cabaret stage, dressed in paper bags or some such, deliberately breaking every rule that established dance audiences expected, pretty costumes, pretty women, clever steps, to melodious music. No.

Laban attended, with his *ménage à trois* household, dancer and pianist Susanne Perrottet and his wife, singer Maja Lederer. In hopeful mood Schwitters arrived, to lend his already anarchic tendencies to the creation of visual objects, Merz objects, collages of found fragments. What connected these two innovators was their insistence on a positive way forward in stark contrast to the Dadaists furious nihilistic response to war, Schwitters to make art out of debris, Laban to open up new modes of expressive human collaborative movement; both carrying a message of hope in a time of apparent catastrophic hopelessness.

So in bomb-scarred Manchester thirty years later the two wounded Titans met again to struggle on, pursuing their positive message in whatever way available, Kurt to create his now famous Merzbarn in a field in the Lake District, Laban to set in place an array of avenues for the study and use of creative movement.

Into this atmosphere I strode, naïve, unprepared, hesitant but focused. Laban saw a useful pawn in this impoverished middle class teenager, a trainable apprentice. Some students he ignored, me he did not. I asked questions, why this and why that. He welcomed curiosity. Throughout the freezing winter of 1946/47 I grew from a sixteen-year-old schoolgirl into something quite else.

If my mother had had any idea what I was coming into she would have blanched for the contrast between a girls' boarding school and 108 Oxford Road was chasmic. To start with I studied with ten others, age range sixteen to forty, from seven countries, a motley crew of men and women all determined to discover the innovations that Rudolf Laban and his assistant Lisa Ullmann could give them. He had been the king of German Expressionist Dance, world famous in 1936, thrown out by the Nazis, now a struggling nobody in post-war Britain.

But we were all struggling, all without means, all facing an unknown future as the world recovered from the horrors of WW2. We all shared a determination to make the world a better place where people cared instead of hated, built instead of knocked down, embraced in place of killing. The sense of hope I felt was a palpable daily experience, new and wondrous, which enabled me to transcend the difficulties that assaulted me.

108 Oxford Road was an office on the first floor over a noisy workshop not even as good or as large as a school gymnasium, and grubby. One gas fire to warm the space was inadequate. We were cold. The changing room was a small dark room, with a gas ring where we brewed tea, along

the corridor a dilapidated loo. So, sweating, we all stripped off together after class. It was the first time I had seen a naked man close to.

Two of us school girls had arrived together. My mother had organised for Maggie, also from Downe House, and me to live in a YWCA. To me it felt like a girls' boarding school and I determined to get out of it. The contrast between what I was discovering by day with the YWCA regime was stark. So out we went onto the back streets of Manchester, we two innocent girls, knocking on doors in the working-class area of Old Trafford asking fearlessly, naïvely, for a room and we found one, in a back-to-back terrace. It could only happen in the extraordinary post-war climate of reconstruction, young people asked for help and adults offered to share what they had. We moved in with an ex-miner, his wife and a granny to a room with a double bed, the loo out in the yard through the kitchen. I need hardly tell you that shortly Maggie's parents removed her so I was on my own.

I had to adjust to so many things that were strange. Mancunian speech of the time was local dialect, older people used thee and thou. I could hardly understand my landlady. 'As't 'ad a pow, luv?' she asked. I discovered she meant had I had a hair cut. 'Tea' was at 5.30, the main meal, then at 9pm the man went out for his fish and chips. The tin bath was put out in the kitchen once a week for all to share, publicly, but that was not enough for a sweaty dancer. The cold tap in the kitchen was all I had for a morning wash. But, heyho, the dancing was fabulous.

I was discovering more than dancing from my fellow students. Take Rita. Thirtyish, brittle, nervous, mid-European, she had lost all her family in Treblinka death camp. For her, dance was a therapy, a hoped-for cleansing, but it didn't work because after she left she committed suicide. Rome, intelligent, sunny girl, well off, in what we would now call her gap year. The male members of Theatre Workshop were her main attraction and I think she went off with one at the end of the year. Ronnie, my age, Scottish, excellent Highland dancer, earned at the local Frascati restaurant, gave me my first inklings into what homosexuality might be. I had never heard of such a thing and of course it was illegal. Mary, thirty-ish, sophisticated performer from an all-black group in France, her partner a photographer on the *Daily Mirror*, a paper forbidden at Downe House. Clare, a dance teacher, soft and expressive with such a strong Derbyshire accent I couldn't understand her at all. Hettie, rising forty, from the Manchester Jewish community, an actress turned dancer, scarily ugly but choreographically talented. Little Lisa, acted as secretary to Ullmann, a German refugee with absolutely no money. One lunchtime I watched her grate a potato and heat it with a spot of lard and we shared it and she had the same for supper.

For them all, expressive dance was what they wanted to do, the only alternative being ballet, tap, or musical comedy, careers for which none of us was suited in body or outlook. Together, with our individuality valued, we collaborated, created, studied and I grew up.

By term two of my training we were rehearsing for a performance, at the first international choreographic competition post war, held in Copenhagen. We were joined by several men from Joan Littlewood's Theatre Workshop, actor/movers of a left-wing persuasion, several being members of the Communist Party. I found myself both performing and in charge of costumes, being deemed responsible. We made them out of net, sacks, military underwear, anything available not on clothes rationing. We rehearsed at all hours, creating, repeating, Laban commanding, Ullmann hovering, Joan Littlewood swearing in the wings, percussing, singing, dancing, sewing. Off we went by ferry and train to Denmark, the first overseas travel for most of us. We were lodged with different families, mine enjoyed sitting in the garden in the nude, another shock. We performed and won a modest commendation.

So ended my first year. I returned home with my head spinning and my heart elated. I knew, hard as it was, that 108 Oxford Road was the place for me, at Laban's side, and nothing my confused family said would change my mind.

Two years later, Kurt Schwitters died. It coincided with my being worn out and needing a break from the rigours of apprenticeship to Laban. He said, 'I pay, you to go to Langdale. Find Schwitters' barn.' All I had gleaned about Schwitters was that he made new art out of rubbish. I took a train to Ambleside in the Lake District en route to Langdale. In the carriage with me was a middle-aged man. He chatted me up, a new experience, and offered me a cigarette. Teenage girl's first puff. I came back from Langdale luckily still a virgin but a smoker. Over the years Laban and I shared many a Wills Woodbine.

Last year, on a Lake District holiday, I searched for the Langdale Inn. It must have been what is now an expensive complex of holiday cottages for on the opposite side of the lane is a gate labelled 'Schwitters Merzbarn, key with porter' or some such remark.

In 1948 there was no gate or key but a meadow and in it a tumbledown barn into which I ventured. It seemed abandoned. Inside strange stuff was plastered on to the walls. It felt unfinished. It smelt dank. I had no conceptual tools to make anything of it. Indeed I disliked its strangeness and its sense of decay and I came away. Today I would have photographed the famous barn from every angle but during the war cameras were forbidden and I had none. Schwitters is now a world-renowned name and some of the Merzbarn is saved as a much-visited museum piece in the University of Newcastle's Hatton Gallery.

Back in Manchester one morning, Laban said in his broken English, 'Go out. Pick up. Bring here. We make.' We scoured the sooty streets of Manchester and returned with bus tickets, cigarette papers, metal fragments, anything that the Mancunian public had thrown in the gutter. And we made collages out of them on newspaper. So is this what the barn was all about? Making a barn an art object with junk? But then he said, 'Go. Watch people. Bring here. We make.' We brought back fragments of behavioural movement, a nod, a greeting, a stance, all manner of mundane throw-away gestures.

We 'collaged' them in sequences and performed them to each other, perhaps one of the first occasions that raw behaviour became dance. I didn't know how to make use of it then but it was a revelation and stuck. Forty years later when remounting Laban's early choreographies formed from behavioural gestures, I knew how to transform them into a performance.

Lisa Ullmann leading class, from l, Meggie Tudor Williams, Mary Elding, VP-D, Warren Lamb, Lisa, Hettie Loman (Ph. Roland Watkins, Laban Collection)

In Copenhagen from L, Sylvia Bodmer, Lisa Ullmann, and fellow dancers Veronica Tyndale Biscoe, Pat Burgess, Mary Elding, Hettie Loman, Fernanda, Maureen Myers

Lisa Ullmann leading a rehearsal
of *The Forest*. (Ph. Roland Watkins,
Laban Collection)

VP-D demonstrating Laban's dance
notation (Ph. Roland Watkins,
Laban Collection)

Ronnie Curran, Rita Hartstein, Rome Bell, VP-D, in Copenhagen.

THE ART OF MOVEMENT STUDIO

183/5 OXFORD ROAD, MANCHESTER, 13
Principal: E. M. M. LISA ULLMANN, L.D., L.M.G.

Modern Educational Dance

Movement and Dance for the Stage

Industrial Rhythm

Two-year graduate course for teachers. Study of bodily technique and the significance of movement in education. Teaching practice.

One-year postgraduate course (for Graduates of AMS only) for trainers of teachers.

One-year supplementary course for teachers whose training has been in two-year or in emergency training colleges. Grant-aided by the Ministry of Education.

Full-time training course in stage movement for dancers and actors.

Courses for Industrial movement trainers. Study of effort and motion in work. Practical application in factories. A limited number of scholarships available from industrial firms.

Examinations. Teaching Certificates. Diplomas.

For further information and application form, apply to the secretary.

The Art of Movement Studio flyer (Laban Collection)

CHAPTER 5

1948

Do it Again

Laban entered my life when he started to look at me as a possible apprentice. Considering our relationship from his perspective, to start with I was of little interest. His passion for promoting dance and movement overwhelmed everything he did. He looked at the people surrounding him only as to how they could support his cause, how they could further one of the branches of his multi-stranded vision.

I observed him gather collaborators: Diana Jordan and Arthur Stone, established practitioners for movement in drama, Joan Goodrich, head of dance at Bedford College of Physical Training, Myfanwy Dewey, His Majesty's Inspector of Schools, educational dance enthusiast, Fred Lawrence, industrial management consultant and friend, John Macmurray, philosopher, visionary, and fellow traveller in egalitarianism, Joan Littlewood, maverick director of experimental Theatre Workshop, Esmé Church, director of Bradford Civic Theatre, promoter of movement in drama.

In addition were several apprentices in their twenties, already in place: Jean Newlove, started as had I as a raw school girl, talented for movement in drama (went on to a life-long career in theatre), Geraldine Stephenson, graduate of Bedford, talented at dance drama, (went on to a life-long career as a solo dancer and as choreographer for television), Veronica Tyndale Biscoe (later Sherborne), graduate of Bedford, interested in movement therapy, (went on to found Sherborne Movement for severely disabled children), Warren Lamb, recently demobbed from the navy, useful for movement in industry (went on to found Movement Profiling and a lifetime career advising industrial management).

These people were all eight or more years older than me, all immediately useful. I was not.

By the beginning of my second year of study, when I was soon to be eighteen, he started to notice me. I was clearly there for a full training, which others were not. I was good at his dance notation while few were, I was quick to understand his ideas on the science and art of movement, I could move well, I was reliable if given a task and I asked questions and demanded answers. The Pilkington Tile Factory assignment was a turning point.

Laban was employed to advise on manual labour, how to increase output in several factories and on the Manchester Ship Canal. Being classified as 'an enemy alien' that is how he was used by the state. He needed assistants at Pilkingtons. He had to use me as I was the only student who had mastered the movement notation, a skill needed to write the tile makers routines. Not only did I go willingly, catching a 6 am train, I did well what he wanted done and I recognised and solved the immediate technical problems of writing workers' actions on a power press in a notation designed for dance. I could see his look change, 'Aha, this child might have something'.

Soon after that he took me aside at the end of the working day. He had been watching the last minutes of an exhausting class taught by Lisa Ullmann. I was about to leave the studio with everyone else, whacked and sweaty when:

'Val,' he said, 'Do it again.' So I went back into the studio and did the phrase again.

'Do it again,' he said. After the fifth demand, indignant, I burst out, 'What do you want?' Probably for the first time in his presence, maybe in my life, I felt physically passionate.

'Ah,' he said. 'Do it again.' Furious I did, dancing it with the dynamism of rage.

'Ah,' he said. 'Tomorrow we work again. Now we have a whisky.'

We did. That was the first time he spoke to me as a fellow-traveller. It was a fateful day for from then on not only was my expressivity as a dancer transformed but my middle-class reserve was irrevocably shed and my life's mission begun. We seldom shared whisky as he rarely drank but we smoked in the garden of his home with Lisa Ullmann hovering, her anxious jealousy never far away. He left me his cigarette lighter in his will. It is in my study behind me as I write.

Eighteenth birthdays are traditionally great opportunities for celebration. Mine was odd. In Manchester after a morning at Pilkington's

Tile Factory and an afternoon of class and rehearsal, I celebrated with fellow student Warren Lamb. This being 1948, strict rationing, and with neither of us having any money, my birthday 'cake' was to be a blancmange, stirred on the ring over Warren's gas fire. What it was made of I have no idea but the packet was not rationed and cost sixpence, threepence each, plus a pint of milk. Neither of us had made blancmange before. It is supposed to turn out like a jelly, stand up on a plate looking, we hoped, cake-shaped.

As we stirred, while looking through our notation notes on the Pilkington tile makers, the mixture did not seem to us to thicken, so we put in a second sachet and stirred on.

It did thicken, to such an extent that the 'cake' had the consistency of concrete. It was quite inedible. Ah well, and we had spent sixpence. Warren did have two pieces of chocolate from his ration, saved for next week. Generous man he gave me one and with a 'happy birthday' greeting, I set off in the dark to walk the two miles to my own digs. Heyho.

My Pilkington's experience reappeared years later in connection with Laban's own choreography. Shortly my colleague Alison Curtis-Jones will rehearse *Green Clowns* or rather *Die Grünen Clowns*, his tragic-satiric suite made in 1928. Created with the Kammertanzbühne Laban, Laban's chamber dance group, the piece was conceived by him and produced by his rehearsal director Dussia Bereska. It is one of the dances I re-found in my researches into Laban's theatre life.

Green Clowns being a work made largely with structured improvisation each performance is a fresh re-creation with the dancers from the known particulars of the structure and with Laban's rehearsal methods. Without my realising it at the time he was using these methods at Oxford Road on us students, in workshops on a choreographed *Magic Flute* and a dynamic study *Chaos Fight and Liberation* and *The Forest*, shown in the Copenhagen Choreographic Competition of 1947. So I knew his creative methods.

In *Green Clowns* we re-create four scenes, *Machine*, *War*, *Romance in Green* and *Eccentrics Club*. Anti-mechanisation is a theme that turns up more than once in Laban's oeuvres. Here the first scene opens with a conveyor belt motif of linked human bodies, kneeling, lurching forward in gross discomfort. The second motif shows workers operating machines in pitiless repetition. In trying to find a way to choreograph such a theme my mind turned to Pilkingtons. There staunch Lancashire women had laboured hour on hour turning sand into tiles on heavy power press machines. They placed each emerging 'tile' on to the moving belt that conveyed them away to be fired, stippled, glazed and boxed up. Some women took 11 seconds to press a tile, some 11.5, novices 13 seconds each 'choreographing' her own version of what had to be done. This phrase and its inhumanity I wrote in detail and it stuck in my mind. I decided to incorporate it in *Green Clowns* 1987, our first re-creation and it has remained in all performances.

Above Rudolf Laban as I first met him (Ph. Hans Tschirren, State Archive Canton Bern)

Left In His Majesty's Inspector Myfanwy Dewey's garden with Veronica Tyndale Biscoe and Fernanda

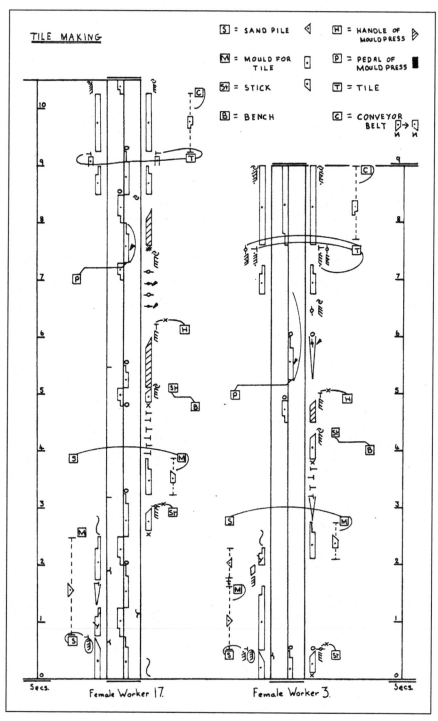

My notation of two workers' phrase at Pilkington's Tile Factory

CHAPTER 6

1948

Getting Home Somehow

Polly, my granddaughter, and Max, both undergraduates, stayed overnight yesterday en route for Paris. Prepared with tent and cycle routes they will pedal to the Eiffel Tower in three days, with no doubt sore bodies and a triumphant heart. My mind went to my longest bicycling adventure entered into not for fun or love but financial necessity.

To pay for my board and lodging as a student my dear mother took in paying guests at £2.00 a week and sent me the cheque to pay my landlady 35/-, all in. That's £1.75 in today's money, leaving me 5/- or 25p for everything else. That was not much for a hungry dancing girl with aspirations and needing lunch. It left nothing to get home with at the end of the term as a train ticket from Manchester to London was £3.00. Two solutions offered, hitch-hike or cycle.

I did hitch, one April, with an actor from Theatre Workshop. My last pennies went on the bus fare to an out-of-town night-time lorry park where we boarded a mammoth vehicle carrying gas stoves to London. Un-roofed, we were open to the elements but the stoves were packed with straw. With some creativity we made a reasonable if prickly space for the two of us to snuggle down, doze and attempt to keep warm and dry. There being no motorways, yet, it was a long night. On arriving home the first action of my mother was to run a bath. She said my skin was grey, ingrained with Mancunian grime and it probably was.

My bike was of the sit-up-and-beg sort with a wicker basket on the handlebars, somewhat rickety from cycling over the cobbled streets of Manchester. Unlike Max's racing model and Polly's student version, mine had no gears. From a morning modelling nude at the art school I had enough cash to buy khaki panniers from the Army Surplus Store to fix over my back wheel in which I packed minimal essentials. To turn necessity into an adventure my sisters rallied, Elizabeth agreeing to meet me at Warwick where Alison was teaching in a girls' boarding school. After scrounging leftovers from her school's kitchen for our supper she guided us to a friendly barn filled with fresh cut hay and we slept our first alfresco night. We awoke bitten all over as the hay was alive with harvest bugs. The farmer's wife covered our spots with soothing bicarbonate of soda and off we went itching as we pedalled.

Sitting on a park bench we planned our sleeping stops, starting with Stratford-on-Avon. Travelling post war was tricky food-wise with nothing available without coupons. One B&B owner at Stratford said, 'You can stay for free in return for your bread coupons. I need them to feed my chickens.' It seemed a fair deal saving us enough pennies to queue for gallery seats at the theatre. Hooray, Shakespeare in exchange for bread coupons. During the war all signposts had been removed to confuse the expected Germans and it took a few years for them to return and some did not. Maps were handed in too, so knowing which road to take was a bit of a gamble. While Polly and Max had a *Cycle Routes in Europe* special booklet to guide them I had found a second hand pre-war atlas and hoped that would serve.

First stop after Stratford was a friendly farm worked by Italian prisoners of war who eyed two nubile girls as manna from heaven. We climbed into the loft, firmly pulled up the ladder and opened our first tin of pilchards, fish being coupon-free but our bread was in the Stratford chicken coop.

Next stop, Ilsom, a very large mansion in Tetbury, being the home of my father's successful brother Sir Walter Preston, industrialist and Tory MP for Cheltenham. His wayward (divorced) and much-admired-by-us sister Auntie Jane, lived in an estate cottage. We were greeted, sweaty and dishevelled, by the butler at Ilsom itself and we handed over the army panniers which were unpacked and laid out on the spotless eiderdowns, revealing all, including a second tin of pilchards. Aunt Ella was not the sort to discourse on existentialism and communism, topics I had learnt to relish from Joan Littlewood and her Theatre Workshop company. Nor were Sir Walter or wicked Auntie Jane. This was a Conservative stronghold with huntin' shootin' fishin' yachtin' the topics. After an awkward dinner served on the left by the said butler, we slept in pristine sheets and departed as dawn rose, seen off by Auntie Jane.

Next stop, Benson on the river Thames, home of an elderly distant cousin, quite mad Aunt Ethel, widow of Cappy Miller, an adventuring seafaring man. She lived in her kitchen covered in coal dust as her house disintegrated round her, apparently happy and quite unconcerned at her dilapidation. In her overgrown kitchen garden we found potatoes. So baked potatoes it was, cooked on her open kitchen grate. No butter of course or cheese or baked beans. Rationed. Upstairs we found a bedstead, sheetless, and slept on that. My long-suffering mother came on a Clean-up-Aunt-Ethel visit twice yearly.

When Ethel died some years later she divided her belongings between her two nieces, one received the dilapidated house and the other, my mother, received shares. Glory of glories, being in property, the shares had grown in value and Nancy, for the first time since Bill's death, had a solvent bank balance.

Next stop Windsor Castle, home of Duncan Armytage, Canon of St George's Chapel where the great and good congregate from time to time in Their Majesties' presence for events of marvellous pomp and circumstance. Auntie Betty, Mrs Armytage, Nancy's stepsister, a cordon bleu cook and hostess, fed us miraculously on, I think, one of Their Majesties' chickens. But even at Royal Windsor they were short of coal, also rationed, so no hot water. Betty considered the incompatability of our muddy state with her sheets so we decided it wiser to sleep on the roof in our army blankets. Rooftops of castles offer unusual and spectacular dawns but also dew. On waking to the tolling bells of Eton College we found ourselves soaking wet. Dried out below we departed for our last forty miles.

We had a £1 note left from our £2 budget. That being to us a lot of money we determined not to break into it. The time of trial came at Walton-on-Thames for our lunch break. We lay the bikes down and washed our feet in the river but the opened tin of pilchards ran into the opened tin of condensed milk, our last. Hungry as we were we could not face that version of hors d'oevres.

We did get home to Nancy's cottage that evening, I pushing the last ten miles with my thighs ablaze from serge shorts scraping sunburned skin. Today Polly and Max rode triumphant round the Eiffel Tower. Over sixty years ago we limped in exhausted, famished, but equally triumphant.

My aunt Jane Pitman in hunting dress, at Ilsom

CHAPTER 7

1949

British Dance Theatre

I am writing on a Great Western train heading for Salisbury where, in the cathedral, we will celebrate, as a family, the end of a responsible year as High Sheriff of Wiltshire of William Wyldbore-Smith, the eldest of my many nephews. And a surprising service it was, combining ceremonial pomp with contemporary opportunity. Since a High Sheriff, in velvet breeches and lace cravat, is there as the Queen's representative to promote the law throughout the county, judges, barristers, bewigged and begowned, mayors and mayoresses from across the county, with chain of office, processed to the nave with Dean and Bishop, choirboys and clergy there to join all manner of great and good souls active in the voluntary services of Wiltshire.

For me the surprise and a silent hooray came with the readings, the first from Exodus telling of the Jewish law, read by the senior judge, the second from the Koran, read by the High Sheriff of Bristol, a Moslem woman, the third from St Mark's gospel presenting the essence of Christian law, read by William. What better way to celebrate the multicultural nature of Great Britain? How good to hear the Bishop of Salisbury preaching on all three readings. My Quaker heart jumped for joy for here was a celebration of equality and symbol of peaceful coexistence, central to Quaker philosophy, in a building long associated with religious division. My father would have hoorayed with me for he, as the father of his Christian flock, championed the working man of whatever creed or race, in multicultural Lewisham.

My mind turned to a very different activity in Salisbury sixty-four years before when with British Dance Theatre I came to the city theatre to perform our avant-garde repertoire to the astounded populace. The company came about in 1949 during my last year as a dance student, led by Hettie Loman, the mature Mancunian actress turned choreographer, of immense imagination, sense of theatre and courageous persistence.

She selected six of us, a mixed bunch, all with a passion to perform, to bring to the public our message, through dance theatre. The archives from Manchester's Library Theatre hold programmes from our first performances there detailing a wide repertoire of serious, amusing, duos, trios and group pieces all conceived and danced in what was then a quite new creative style, bringing a fresh form of dance theatre to ballet-dominated Britain. We were well received by the theatre press but the ballet critics were, as expected, unenthusiastic.

Two duos I remember clearly perhaps because of their stark contrast. *Born of Desire* focused on the internal struggle of a childless couple danced with dramatic pathos against Grieg's lamenting sound. I was too young to do it justice I imagine but my partner Warren Lamb, ten years my senior, brought the gravitas it needed. *Pleasure Spent* I danced in red skirt and yellow socks with Ronnie Curran, fellow teenager, and we were right for it, jitterbugging in 'morning after the night before' mood with Duke Ellington to give us the jazzy tension.

These short but pithy duos interspersed our main works many of which were social comments on post-war culture. One that seemed to speak to the audience was a trio, *Once I Had Laughter* for two men, one young, the other mature and a woman. The drama unfolded as each character struggled with the memories of the concentration camp where they had suffered. For Hettie, from a Jewish family, the theme was especially vivid. This was 1950, only four years after the photographs of Belsen and Auschwitz had burst on to our newspapers in sickening and deeply shocking images.

The immediate post-war years held a plethora of themes for all creative artists and we expressionist dancers were in the thick of it, with Joan Littlewood's Theatre Workshop rehearsing just round the corner experimenting, as were we, with a 'What Now?' question. It was a time of deep austerity, we none of us possessed anything, living on meagre food in unheated digs in smog-filled Manchester. Clothes were rationed, meat, cheese, coal, sweets, bread, everything was rationed. To keep our dancers' legs warm we bought cheap army surplus long johns, unrationed, and attempted to disguise their origin by dyeing them black. We made costumes out of air force surplus parachute silk, unrationed. This was of course a pre-nylon era.

Streets Without End was a dance of Hettie's for a larger group, dealing with backstreet poverty and unemployment. I recall the main character, a man in cloth cap, while I was attempting and failing to create a crippled child. Laban saw a rehearsal and came over as I struggled. He tore two large pieces of paper from a ledger. He placed one between my knees and one between my elbow and ribs. 'Now dance', he said. It was so simple and so effective. No reliance on fake emotion or imagination, just physical incapacity for real.

My first choreographic effort at this time was with a Youth Club in Stockport, a disparate group of teenage boys and girls, sixteenish, who had never performed before.

Like *Streets Without End* the theme I chose was of the time, a group of refugees floundering in post-war Europe. The miracle for us young choreographers was the emergence of 78 rpm records. You went to a music shop and were able to take five discs into a booth and listen until you heard something that might work for your choreography. For me the growling jazz of Stan Kenton hit the nail. The youth clubbers loved it, as something quite new but relevant and of 'now'. Miraculously, they entered into the dramatic spirit of the narrative and together we made a success of the performance.

Upper right Hettie Loman's *Born of Desire*, with Warren Lamb

Lower right Hettie Loman's *Pleasure Spent*, with Ronnie Curran

Hettie Loman's *Streets Without End*, (?), Joan Russell, Sally Archbutt, Warren Lamb with VP-D on the floor

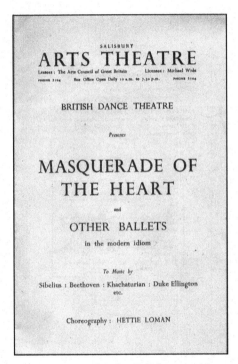

British Dance Theatre's programme for the Salisbury performances

CHAPTER 8

1951

Making a Start

I am in a box at the Royal Festival Hall, in my customary seat. Today it is Benjamin Britten's *War Requiem* that I know so well with its texts from the war poets and angelic boys' choir. It was at Oxford Road that I first encountered 20th century music up front and close. Britten was one of the composers, not yet fully established. Eric Styles was our pianist, but since money was short little went on musicians, rather on a gas fire in the arctic conditions of a Manchester winter. I recall creating a study, possibly my first, probably awful. I added Debussy's *Clair de Lune*, new to me, but in the version arranged for Mantovani Strings. Laban gently suggested if I were going to include music it is as well to know the original. Oh dear. But I was only sixteen and did not possess a wind-up gramophone.

My first encounter with the Festival Hall was as a costumier. The title Festival refers to the Festival of Britain of summer 1951, with its Skylon and Dome of Discovery, designed to give a lift to the war weary, rationing weary, populace. The newly built Festival Hall hosted a season by the Festival Ballet, the company that metamorphosed later into English National Ballet, but led in 1951 by Anton Dolin and Alicia Markova with impresario Julian Braunsweg. I was performing when I could with British Dance Theatre but making ends meet by any means including assisting with the two toddlers of Kate Austin, erstwhwile stage director for Ballets Jooss, now living in Knightsbridge. She had seen our performance at the small Park Lane Theatre.

Knowing we were struggling financially Kate offered to house me in return for child care. That included scrubbing their front doorstep in Brompton Square. Part of my job was to mask the truth that they too, Kate and her Norwegian husband, were as hard up as us dancers, although they lived in Knightsbridge. Lodging with them was her sister, Nan Austin, ballet costumier, who slept in the dining room, and a gaunt woman in fashion who had rented the drawing room. I slept in the attic alongside two recovering refugees.

Nan had a feisty relationship with rival costumier Madame Beriosova, wife of Festival Ballet's ballet master, but she hoped nevertheless to get some work for the opening season at the Festival Hall. She did, and needed an assistant, alias dog's-body. So I obliged. In between ballet class at the School of Russian Ballet in Chelsea (which I paid for by teaching my fellow students notation) and changing the nappies of the Austin children, I learnt the rudiments of the costumier's trade.

This being a fairly new post-war ballet company only a sparse wardrobe existed. A good deal had to be made from scratch. With no upfront finance, fabrics could not be bought until tickets started to sell. That left us and Madame Beriosova with minimum time to costume three ballets with a large corps de ballet as well as soloists. A tall order. The *Polovtsian Dances* from *Prince Igor* with Roerich designs was one, Michael Charnley's new work *Symphony for Fun* was another with the traditional Christmas ballet, *The Nutcracker,* the third.

A modern basement studio in Yeoman's Row was where we cut, painted, stitched. It consisted of one large room, cobalt blue, lime green and white, with loo and gas ring. Just down the Row lived Frederick Ashton whose neat patent leather shod feet we saw passing above.

I had never made a tutu in my life, but instructed by an experienced seamstress I eventually clocked up five in an eighteen-hour day working on a treadle sewing machine. We bought yards of cotton material from Berwick Street, the hub of theatrical fabrics, for the baggy trousers for *Prince Igor.* Every inch had to be painted in stripes to follow the Roerich designs. That was my job, painting all night through, in suffocating fumes.

The Charnley piece needed twelve women and twelve men in three colour groups each graduated from strong to pale, according to the designs by young Australian Tom Lingwood. My task was to organise the shades in an incredible dyeing shop in Maida Vale. Yards and yards of white material were dipped in huge vats, some for a short time, some for longer. Did the gradation succeed first time? No it did not, So back to Berwick Street to buy more yards while Nan negotiated extra finance with Braunsweg.

Dancers turned up for fittings, just the bodices for the Charnley piece and just the four inch basques for the tutus, made expertly by Nan. After the fittings I added the layers of tulle frills. The basque must fit absolutely to the dancer's physique. It must feel right. I just held the pins and Nan coped with the temperaments. One ballet required a headdress, was it for a princess or a swan? With a five-minute instruction it was mine to create with wire, gauze, net, feathers and an array of bling. I admit to having been quite pleased with it. Surely not for Markova, that was Madame Beriosova's domain, mine graced a lesser soloist of some sort, probably the young Belinda Wright.

The show was due to get in on Boxing Day. How many nights we worked right through I can't remember, but they were many. That Christmas Eve was memorable. We worked in the studio till 11pm then slipped into Brompton Oratory for midnight mass, ate Christmas dinner at the house at 1am, then back to the studio till dawn. After a couple of hours sleep on the floor we decamped everything to the Festival Hall in a series of cabs and set up a workroom and wardrobe in a space behind the Royal Box.

Our problem was the gold paint, needed for what defeats my memory but we had to apply gold dust with alcohol, naturally hallucinogenic. We took it in turns to take a break every ten minutes to come back to earth dashing to the Royal Box, breathing deeply, then back to the fumes. When it came to the Charnley premiere the girls had to be sewn in. We just had not managed to machine on the tapes of hooks and eyes so needle and thread it was as the five-minute call rang out.

In the interval this evening, before Britten's *War Requiem* my eye was drawn to the Royal Box opposite. I am eating an ice cream such as I could never have afforded in 1952, nor would one have been available in that time of rationing and austerity. But I do recall one afternoon when with pride and joy and a shilling in my pocket I met my sister Elizabeth in a café in the middle of the Festival precinct and could afford to buy her a bun and a cup of tea, thanks to Mr Braunsweg.

The season ended and I returned to more dance, rehearsals, performances and nappies, learning tap and stage at a studio in Upper Brook Street in return for a modern class. From time to time just to see if they can, my eighty-year old feet give a shuffle-tap-step-ball-change, and they can.

Into London came one of the first American musicals, *Kiss Me Kate*, the song and dance version of Shakespeare's *The Taming of the Shrew* with dances by Agnes de Mille. Every dancer in town wanted to be in it. I went along for an audition but was hopelessly outclassed. However, I met up with Ann Hutchinson, one of de Mille's assistants who had written the choreography in Labanotation. I believe it was the first copyrighted dance score for the commercial theatre.

I receive a Christmas card each year from Ann and her husband Ivor Guest or rather an illustrated round robin of their jet-setting lifestyle even though both of them are in their nineties. Some years ago on one of my visits to their apartment in Holland Park I was interested to see that their dining-room table, sitting room, spare bed, hallway, were strewn with manuscripts as both of them prepared books, Ivor on the Romantic Ballet and Ann on the Language of Dance, alias notation. Looking at the relative calm of my study, even if my dining table is piled high, my bedroom has not yet succumbed to paper as I fear Ann and Ivor's had.

Being full of verve for the publicity of the notation system, having successfully opened the Dance Notation Bureau in New York, Ann was all set to take London by storm by hosting lecture demonstrations. She needed a demonstrator. Enter Valerie, an equally competent notator. Just where and to whom we demonstrated I cannot recall except one event in the English Speaking Union to which the ballet community had been invited.

The format was that Ann would introduce the symbols of Labanotation and I embody them. I would then leave the room, an audience member obliged with a dance phrase that Ann would notate on a blackboard for all to see, whereupon in I came, read it and danced it. Applause. Of course today we have computerised ways of writing dance scores but in London in the early 1950s Xerox machines were not yet invented. Every bit of notation was written by hand and copied by hand.

These demonstrations bore fruit for before long I found myself in the lower echelons of the Royal Opera House secretly giving notation lessons to Mary Skeaping, ballet mistress extraordinary. Under no circumstances was Madame, Ninette de Valois, to know about this assignation, quite why was never clear to me. However, secrecy was maintained. As history will show Labanotation was not Dame Ninette's ultimate choice. The

Royal Ballet today employs a choreologist to record new works in Benesh notation which actually is ideally suited to the genre.

From time to time during my meetings with Mary Skeaping her brother joined us. Perhaps you have seen John Skeaping's famous drawings of horses. He had a habit of embracing a young woman and carting her off, which he did me, luckily not to his flat in Praed Street but to a night club in Soho. Was it the Flamingo in Leicester Square or Club Eleven in Windmill St? Somewhere where Ronnie Scott played alluring jazz. John could dance and so could I. He could drink and I learned to. Luckily I had other night-time assignments to go to rather than Praed Street for another of my notation challenges was to arrive at the Leicester Square Empire around midnight to meet the choreographer of the elaborate dance shows there. Cine Variety was an evening with film sandwiched between shows danced by scantily clad girls in marvelously synchronised numbers.

The choreographer, Alan Carter, was having difficulty in remembering the steps and also running out of fresh ideas. He wanted a script to remind him what he had done in the past and could resurrect. I think I gave him two notation sessions but a fatal flaw emerged. Dance notation records what each dancer actually does from their perspective. Alan watched always from the front of house and wanted a means to recall what he saw, the overall directorial view, which is another thing altogether than a performer's score. So I couldn't help him and had to find other excuses to circumvent Praed Street.

Above Ann Hutchinson (Guest) teaching notation at Jacob's Pillow, 1953.
(Ph. John Lindquist, © Harvard Theatre Collection)

Below Festival Ballet's *Polovtsian Dances* from *Prince Igor*, the men wearing the
striped trousers. (Ph. Paul Wilson, Courtesy English National Ballet).

CHAPTER 9

1952

A Hard Lesson

Living in an attic and nominally caring for two toddlers was preferable to an unlit cellar underneath the studio hired for class and rehearsals of British Dance Theatre. The room is still there in Westbourne Grove, round the corner from Paddington Station. As it was the only accommodation on offer four of us dancers dossed down there. Ronnie had acquired a camp bed but we three girls, Meg Tudor Williams, Joan Carrington and I, shared a bedstead and a carpet. The gas and electricity had not been paid by the previous occupants. When in residence we sat in candlelight eating kippers, cheap and needing no cooking. Ah well, what one put up with for art!

It was from here that we rehearsed for one of the first dance performances on TV. Recently I rehearsed for a current performance, BBC4's 'Dance Rebels', two rehearsals for two BBC programmes, sixty-five years apart. The contrast between the one and the other is stark, the state of the art light, sprung floored, mirrored studios of Trinity Laban 2015 or the Westbourne Grove's dingy space 1950. But in its time, mere as it was, it served its purpose within our meagre budget.

Alexandra Palace in north London was the BBC's early television home. TV viewing was minute in those days, very few people had a set, and there was no programme choice. Beaming from Ally Pally started in the evening, daily, not before. Performances took place in one studio, far too small for dance, filmed with one fixed camera centre front and broadcast live. 'Could we take that on', we were asked. You bet we could even with all its hazards. Make-up for black and white television (colour TV didn't exist yet) meant your face, for some reason, was plastered with deep yellow grease paint.

We included Hettie Loman's *Masquerade of the Heart*, a romantic tragedy. We were used to performing with 78rpm records, here the live orchestra was in another space, the sound beamed in the round. Christian Simpson's directorial voice boomed from somewhere, 'Miss Preston stand by for action'...ten, nine, eight... three, two, one.

I started as an old lady shrouded in a grey cloak remembering her wedding day that, predictably, went horribly wrong as the groom went off with the bridesmaid. The Khachaturian score gave us plenty of opportunity for spirited dancing, clandestine whispering, lifts and falls all taking place swooping through the minute triangle of the camera's sight lines. But it worked, the press were kind and gave the fledgling company a boost.

Transition images between one programme's end and the start of another were newly made for each event in those days. 'Any ideas for the lead in?' we were asked. I produced an icosahedron made of elegant wooden dowels which Christian Simpson hung from the ceiling of a light box. 'Twirl it,' he said so I did and that constituted the transition over which an announcer told the viewer what to expect.

Since I was about to be twenty-one, a celebration was mooted but where? Staying temporarily at the time in a West Hampstead basement flat, perhaps dossing down would be a better way of putting it, I was living a disparate life between two worlds, dance world whenever possible but slipping back to my mother's cottage in Surrey when the money ran out. Culturally the pull between the values I loved from working with Laban, classless, egalitarian, free love, radical politics, radical dance, on the one side, and middle-class, conservative, Christian-based human kindness on the other was uncomfortable.

My sweet mother desperate to do her best for her youngest daughter but at her wits end to understand what I was up to, suggested a modest twenty-first event, a sherry party, perhaps. Oh my God, I thought, Hettie, Warren, Ronnie, down here for sherry? Unthinkable. Perhaps it would be better in London, my mother suggested. At all events she kindly bought me two bottles of sherry, an expensive cost for her, and I returned with them to British Dance Theatre's studio. Come my birthday, after a performance at the tiny Embassy Theatre, the bemused audience were offered a drop of sherry in tumblers nicked from the bar and my coming of age was celebrated.

Then, back to Brompton Square. It was Kate Austin who suggested

I go over to Germany, to Essen, where Kurt Jooss and his dance theatre company Ballets Jooss had just returned, Jooss having spent the war years in Britain and his company members in South America. Going to Germany in those days was far from simple. No Easy Jet flip. You needed permissions and papers attached to your passport for each border, French money to cross the channel to Boulogne, Belgian money to pass through Brussels and a German visa plus Deutschmarks.

I made a nightmare freezing cold journey in January 1952 by ferry and two overnight trains, utterly full, so I sat on my luggage in the corridor. I arrived at Essen Hauptbahnhof at 4am in complete darkness, hungry and frozen. I could not believe my eyes as the dawn light revealed the shattered city. Not a single building was intact. The shock was profound. Then out of the cellars people appeared, starting the day, going to work. Only then did I get an intimation of what I might be coming to.

Where in 1951 dance was just beginning to re-emerge from the ashes of the war, Kurt Jooss had been offered a directorship at the Folkwanghochschule to restart the Dance Department that he had led before he fled in 1934, with his revived company Ballets Jooss in residence. Also restarted was the Tanzschreibstube (Dance Notation Institute) run by Albrecht Knust. I conferred with Laban. 'You go,' was his view. So here I was, half of me already regretting my decision.

Ann Hutchinson had given me £10 as I had no money nor had my mother, and I now clutched it in French, Belgian, German cash. It was to enable me to get to Essen and live on for a month or two. If, on that freezing morning, there had been a buffet I would have bought a cup of tea. There was nothing on Essen Hauptbahnhof.

When I reached the Folkwangschule it was clear they were not expecting me. Knust found me a room in a new-build suburb. I climbed an icy hill passing the horse abattoir, two bloody heads on the sidewalk. My room was heated by a coke '*offen*' but being a foreign visitor I had no coke allowance. I was supposed to cook on the *offen* so no warmth, no hot food or drink. The washbasin in the corner was frozen solid. My German was a poor schoolgirl version so I realised I was in a mess. But so were most people in post-war Germany so I decided to make the best of it.

I began work with Albrecht Knust, notator extraordinary. He had drafted an *Abriss*, a German textbook, with copious notation examples.

He needed an English version so we set about it. He had drawn in ink the meticulous notation examples, one hundred and two pages of them each page with five carbon copies underneath sandwiched by black carbon sheets. We had to find the translation to fit the small space beside each example and I would type it in over the five carbon copies.

Knust's name, translated, means crust, and that is what he was, a crusty professor of the most precise sort linguistically with very little English. We struggled to understand each other let alone agree a text. I wondered how long I could take this. But he did buy me a hot meal once a week and was as kind as he knew how to be. He was in any case shattered by the war and was paid a very meagre salary. The saving grace was attending class led by Kurt Jooss. His technique was strange to me at first, it seemed a kind of fluid ballet. I could do it but not well. In the Eukinetics (rhythm) and Choreutics (form) classes I was on known territory so flew with the rest of the dancers. Soon I was asked to attend company rehearsals with the intention that I notate Jooss's new choreographies as he made them. *Weg im Nebel* was the new piece, *Journey in the Fog*. Jooss was struggling with it, changing his mind with every other phrase so I was rubbing out more than I was writing.

In truth Jooss found it extremely difficult to start again creatively in Germany having not experienced the horrors of the bombing and the fighting as had his public. Indeed anyone connected with Britain was still 'the enemy', German dance students did not speak to me. In the street I was stared at, I dressed differently, I looked alien. I certainly smelt different for the local dancers' idea of hygiene was not mine. Nobody shaved their armpits and anti-perspirants were not the norm.

My diet was dire, carrots, black bread, cold acorn coffee and *speck*, which is lumps of cheap fat bacon, eaten in my freezing room. Rationing was as bad in Essen as in London but here I did not have a ration card. Surprisingly one *conditorei* opened with the first post-war cream cakes. They were devoured by local women every afternoon as a heaven-sent release from the austerities of war. However, they were not within my budget even though Knust paid me a modest hourly rate.

One evening I was encouraged to visit Dusseldorf where the repaired opera house was showing Carl Orff's *Carmina Burana* in a new production choreographed by Yvonne Georgi. At the time I had never heard of her but she was the 1930s partner to famous Harald Kreutzberg and like every German artist who had lived through the Nazi period she was trying to get her career together again. On one of my later fact-finding trips to Germany when I began writing Laban's biography, I had asked questions, as one would, to find out what went on under the Nazis. Dance archivist Kurt Peters advised me, 'Don't ask for we won't tell.' The dance community had variously collaborated or gone underground, emigrated or been enlisted into the forces. The pain and regret were palpable.

Dusseldorf on that evening looked flourishing to me, with shops well lit. I only gradually realised that what I saw were ground floor shop fronts only and above were the ruined floors and jagged skyline, as in Essen. I was deeply shocked at the bizarre façades, brave as they were. The experience has never left me.

'Karnival' is strong in the Ruhr country, the festivity in the winter months before Lent. My landlady's family celebrated loudly every weekend, singing and drinking beer. Her husband had recently been demobbed from the army. They invited me down occasionally and I did my best. Their jokes were clearly riotously droll for laughter ricocheted round the *Kuche*, the actions that went with them were coarse in the extreme to me with breasts and penises rather readily taking part. But I did get a hot cup of acorn coffee and once a schnapps.

I worked on at the Folkwang with what opportunities were available to me but my mental and physical health was struggling with isolation, malnutrition and the beginning signs of frostbite. I think it was the last days of the *Karnival* festival that finished me off.

Alteweibstag or Old Wives Day on *Rosen Montag* preceded Shrove Tuesday, England's pancake day, before Ash Wednesday when the forty days of Lent fasting begin. On *Alte Weibstag* the men dress up wearing grotesque masks of wizened old hags. Carrying staffs or whips they have a great time harassing women through the streets. The mayhem ended by my being gathered up by a group of young people to a garret of some kind where everyone appeared to expect you to have sex copiously. The whole thing was the last straw and defeated, I sent a telegram to my mother. I got back to England and my mother's welcoming cottage and on to hospital to alleviate the frostbite, with Knust's translations to finish in my luggage. Ah well, an education but a hard one.

A year later the Ballets Jooss had a short tour of the UK planned. I must have made an impression of some sort while in Essen for Jooss sent a telegram, the way for speedy communication that preceded email, to ask me to join them, in what capacity was unclear. Of course I accepted but the tour was horribly cut short when we were in Leeds. Essen council was unable to support the company financially any more so abruptly the tour was abandoned and everyone made their own way home. The question for me was: where was home?

The thought of retreating to my mother was out, no, no, no, for, bless her, she could not fathom why I put myself through these traumas. So to Manchester I went, to Laban. 'I have no job and no home,' I said. 'Stay wiz me,' he said, so I moved in.

We made an interesting version of a *ménage à trois* as Laban lived with Lisa Ullmann and she was a jealous woman. Laban was exquisitely naughty for Lisa was attempting to steer the Art of Movement Studio into financial security by embracing dance as a creative education and training students as creative dance teachers. In a morally conservative climate her relationship with Laban was seen as tricky. The phrase 'living together' and 'in sin' came rather readily to H.M. Inspector's lips though to my knowledge there was no 'sin' about it. Lisa pressed Laban to marry her but he would have none of it saying he was not free. Well, he had been married to singer Maja Lederer but he failed to divulge to Lisa that they were divorced so he was in fact available for her marital chains. Add a nubile young woman to the *ménage*, me, and the Education Authorities quivered with anxiety.

He was an awful tease. *Meine hausfrau*, he remarked to me behind Lisa's back. Housekeeper indeed she was but bread-winner also. We survived together for three months, Lisa using me to teach technique classes.

Come August we all shifted south to an estate in Weybridge. The Elmhirst family of Dartington had bought Laban a vacant school and we set about transforming the spaces into a dance-friendly venue, the new home of the Art of Movement Studio. My mother's sewing machine was shipped in and I became a curtain maker. So for me began, with the beginning of the new academic year, a chequered stint of eight years as a trainer of dance teachers.

v Ballets

THE BRITISH DANCE THEATRE

itish Dance Theatre has its home at the Art of Movement studio in Manchester.
it performance in London was on television on September 18. It is likely that
any may give some performances in a London theatre in the very near future.
ortance of this company is that it perpetuates the technique founded on the
of the famous modern dance creator, Rudolph Von Laben. One of his most
pupils, Liza Ullman, started the school and Hettie Loman is carrying on the work.

Above: Joan Carrington and Ronnie Curran in the Masquerade of the Heart. *Choreography by Hettie Loman to music of Khachturian's* Gayeneh Suite

Below: Clare Summer as the Flirt and Ronnie Curran as the Delinquent in Hettie Loman's Streets without end *to the music of Revualtas, Sibelius, and Britten*

Sally Archbutt as the Daughter, Curran as the Son, and Valerie as the Mother in Hettie Loman's The Divided *to Samuel Barber music*

Below: Ronnie Curran and Warren Lamb in the Song of the Earth, *which has choreography by Hettie Loman and music to Bach's Toccata and Fugue in A*

nd in the distance
heard his footsteps
slowly fade
nd knew the sudden relaxation
of the stubborn will"

" I drank deep from the rich brown earth.
Listened to its laughter and felt good.
Saw the birth of wheat-gold burst their
  seed soon after,
And life swelled strong where I stood."

thirteen

Dance and Dancers spread for British Dance Theatre's television performance.
(Courtesy Peter William's estate)

Hettie Loman's *Masquerade of the Heart*, VP-D cast as The Bride, with Ronnie Curran as The Bridegroom

Left Albrecht Knust, director of the Tanzschreibstube at Essen

Below My mother's welcoming telegram

Below Kurt Jooss's telegram for the 1953 English tour

Telegramm **Deutsche Bundespost**

95 ✳

aus 23⁹⁵ /22 BOSTON LINCOLNSHIRE 14 22 0920 =

Aufgenommen					Übermittelt	
Tag:	Monat:	Jahr:	Zeit:		Tag:	Zeit:
					an:	durch:

von: durch:

Amt Essen-Werden

PRESTON

FOLKWANGSCHULE

22A ESSEN – WERDENGERMANY =

LOVE AND HOT WATER AWAIT YOU AT BERKLEY COTTAGE =

·MAMA +

Charges to pay
s. d.
RECEIVED

POST 👑 OFFICE

No. 157
OFFICE STAMP

TELEGRAM

Prefix. Time handed in. Office of Origin and Service instructions. Words.

At 12 12 p m CR. 5288 Essen F. 5994 26 27 11 50 At

From TW *delivet after 4 50 pm* To

By

TO { ELT Valerie Preston Berkley Cottage Lingfield

Would you be well enough and free
to go with English tour mid February
till end May Please wire Jooss

For free repetition of doubtful words telephone "TELEGRAMS ENQUIRY" or call, with this form, at office of delivery. Other enquiries should be accompanied by this form and, if possible, the envelope
B or C

CHAPTER 10

1954

Earls Court Road

I have returned from Eastbourne, from a funeral, of Hilary Corlett. My son Roger was there, her godson, and Tina and Ros Rosewarne, daughters of our mutual friend Margaret Rosewarne. I gave the eulogy remembering how I met Hilary at the Art of Movement Studio in its new location in Weybridge.

She being a Physical Education college lecturer was sent to learn what creative dance for children entailed. I was her teacher, almost ten years her junior, with no knowledge of educational principles or experience of teaching children. But I could dance, creatively and dramatically, and choreograph. Laban's ideas were the buzz, and I had an advantage over my peers being almost the only student to have completed his three year training at Oxford Road, if you like the only one to put up with its demands and idiosyncrasies and to have been close to 'the master' throughout. A performing career, albeit short, and a few more life experiences than most, gave my work an edge.

This mix had made me an attractive person to hire by the dance education community. Looking through the archive of letters of the 1950s I see I guest taught all over the UK, Worcester Training College, Birmingham Dance Club, Nonington College, Bedford College... In truth it was the blind teaching the blind for I had never taught children, had no wish to, and yet was training people who would do just that.

Hilary was typical of the learners at the Weybridge studio, Physical Education lecturers, sent to study the dance curriculum of the time, Modern Educational Dance. One, very able woman and experienced, threatened me on her arrival, 'Don't think you can teach me anything,' implying 'you whipper-snapper'. 'We'll see, shall we?' I replied. And I did teach her something but it was not easy. These men and women were all paid their full salary to learn, but I was paid a pittance for the financial state of the Weybridge studio was precarious, it was just hanging on.

We were an interesting team of young teachers, Marion North, ambitious, trained educator but no dancer who would go on to an astounding administrative career as Director of Trinity Laban Conservatoire. Geraldine Stephenson, solo performer, pianist, the most experienced of us three who had been shadowing Laban's drama teaching for some years. Both were my senior by some years. We were colleagues, not friends, teaching and co-working as apprentices each helping Laban with a particular part of his current endeavours. Marion focused on personality assessment through behaviour patterns, Geraldine on training actors and covering when he was too ill to teach.

Laban was working unenthusiastically on a book on his notation. He had to get it in print to protect his copyright before Ann Hutchinson published hers. So I more or less took his notes and wrote it for him. Crusty Knust plied me with letters from Essen full of technical notation issues typed on the utility buff-coloured paper that was still the post-war norm for Germany. As did Ann from New York on blue airmail paper with her conflicting technical views. Laban raised his eyebrows. 'You do it,' he said, meaning find a text for his book that won't offend these two notation afficionados. I did my best.

One student, William Elmhirst, who would later prove a loyal supporter of my creative work, was in fact far more than a student. He was the youngest son of philanthropists Dorothy and Leonard Elmhirst of Dartington Hall and had bought the Weybridge Estate for Laban, his first personal philanthropic act. Of course none of us had any knowledge of his kindness, he was just Bill, a bit shy, treated like any other student. Years later we knew each other well, each of us pursuing our own quest, spurred on by a common bond of gratitude to the man who had given each of us a vision of possibilities.

As ever, Lisa Ullmann disliked her younger colleagues working closeted with Laban. The green-eyed monster of jealousy struck her hard. So it was not long before she encouraged me to accept a post offered at a college. She could see that Laban enjoyed my company as we laughed and smoked together. I accepted the job, to lead the dance at Dartford College of Physical Education.

I took a flat in London, a somewhat out-of-date conversion with a bath in the kitchen, but it was mine. For the first time with a reasonable salary in my pocket and a car, I relished the sweetness of having been, as it were, headhunted, a new experience. I drove to Dartford every day with Michael, a talented pianist. There we made art and the students loved it. A few months ago a year group celebrated their 50th birthday as Dartford alumnae and decided to have it at Trinity Laban to include me in their partying. They remembered a forty-minute piece we had made together, with spoken text from Victor Gollancz, T. S. Eliot, Rumi, Ezra Pound and fragments of Shostakovich, Vivaldi, Carl Orff and silence. It was a journey from chaos, through travail and love to return 'to know the place for the first time'. Yes, it was good to recall our creativity, their learning, and the piece.

152 Earls Court Road offered me a safe haven from which to fly and fly I did. Looking back on it now how I never came to grief was a miracle. I had made a good friend of Margaret Rosewarne, from Bedford PE College and we lived it up every weekend, mostly with medical students. Margaret was a blonde bombshell who attracted men like a magnet. We travelled together sometimes as a foursome, we skiied together, she far better than I, we partied. But we also thought and discussed and planned professionally.

I was attracted to Margaret because of her intellect. She was studying for a Master's degree at Cambridge Institute of Education and I was beginning to write a *Handbook for Modern Educational Dance*. For the first time my lack of formal education was a stumbling block, no serious studying of anything but dance since leaving school at sixteen, plenty of life experiences but insufficient breadth of conceptual language. Margaret had it and was acquiring more. She was in demand too to teach gymnastics on educational holiday courses. As a term ended we would resort to some pleasant location, teach our courses and live it up with the other, male, tutors. Oh dear.

A tinge of desperation coloured my partying, a front. I was in truth deeply attached to Laban, an unhealthy mix of amour and father figure. I could neither acknowledge it nor forget it, but simply deny it and carry on. Margaret understood and went along with the charade.

Surprising people stayed at 152, one was Cousin Helen, my mother's contemporary. As teenagers they had leant against the gatepost after school discussing life and teachers and boys and sex, so my mother told me years later. This in itself was way beyond the norm for sex was never mentioned in those days, girls were not supposed to know what it was let alone try it out. Their ways parted, my mother to become the wife of a bishop, Helen eventually to marry a doubtful millionaire and live on a yacht moored outside Cannes.

One day, on board, sipping champagne with salmon sandwiches, the millionaire said, 'That, my dear, is my last franc.' He had lost it all in the casino. They returned to England, to Cornwall where she had grown up. My mother said, 'Go down to St Ives, look for a teashop, see if you can find Helen.' I motored down and far from finding a teashop I found a steak joint. Helen was front of house, an amazing redhead, achieved through craft and skill for she was seventy if she was a day. Her man, somewhat the worse for wear, was in the back grilling the steaks. He did not last very long so Helen, homeless, came temporarily to 152 Earls Court Road. She plastered the walls of my tiny spare room with glamorous photographs of herself when young. I witnessed her make up, for it took her a full hour, donning the tan cream she smothered on her exposed skin to hide the wrinkles. At a distance she looked forty, and a distance she always kept.

Back at Dartford, I earned my living, collaborating musically with Michael and battling it out with the principal, Miss Edith Alexander. One of my worrisome responsibilities was guiding students through teaching practice. There we were in the dining hall of a primary school with thirty little people, the student attempting to organise their energy in the proposed activity. Some did well and some were awful, and I knew it was partly my fault. I did not know how to prepare them adequately for schoolwork.

To Alexander I went with the hope of getting some advice. Experienced colleagues knew how to organise a gymnasium or a game of hockey. Maybe they could advise on basic skills so I asked Alexander for a lead. Her reply shocked me to the core. 'I don't keep a dog and bark myself,' she said. I suppose in her defence she had no idea how to help me, but what a way to deal with a young teacher. What a contrast to going to Laban to ask his advice. He would listen and with tender care guide one in whatever direction was possible. From that moment on I knew a women's PE College was the wrong place for me and I put in my resignation before the year was out, but it was not accepted. I was upgraded to Senior Lecturer. So I carried on.

Another visitor to 152 came from my wider family, Auntie Betty, the widow of the canon of Windsor (on whose roof I had slept with Elizabeth). She needed a discreet spot to facilitate her courtship by the Bishop of Bath and Wells away from the prying eyes of the hopeful matrons of Wells. You may have seen him standing beside our young Queen in Westminster Abbey in the film of her coronation, a portly, kindly man but not good looking. Betty had cared for his wife in her last illness and he, being a vigorous man, needed a new wife and hostess. I would vacate my flat for a night or two, provide a key, say nothing, as the ecclesiastic endeavour was pursued.

My mother and I witnessed their marriage, a clandestine affair at dawn, held in the private chapel of the bishop's moated palace in Wells. We arrived in the dark, were let in over the drawbridge, gave our signatures to the two minute ceremony, sped the love birds on their way. They were in France before the *Evening Standard* had it all over the front page.

Shortly after, I was called on to help in a culinary emergency. The colours of the Somerset regiment were being furled at the Cathedral followed by a luncheon at the palace. But Betty had succumbed to flu. Could I stand in, supervise the meal and appear on the dais to receive the standard? I was confronted by an already printed menu with *canard á la crème* and other delights that I had no idea how to cook. First call, to catch twelve ducks on the moat and deprive them of life. With the palace team we did it, *crème brûlée* and all and I duly stood as instructed with the Lord Lieutenant at my side as we sang the National Anthem and praised the Almighty. As visions of other less salubrious events of my life passed through my mind I was glad of my facility as a performer.

In 1958 Laban died. It was awful. Many people devoted to his work were devastated. Lisa Ullmann was distraught, the funeral grotesque. For some inexplicable reason she chose a regular Church of England burial service. Why? To my knowledge he was neither atheist nor theist, definitely no Christian worshipper. With the church crowded to standing we got through it and I fled. The thought of the man being lowered into the ground, buried, was too much. I howled like a dog, raising my cries to the cosmos. Oh God, Oh God. I could not tell anyone of my distress. Then back to Dartford, smiling students, keen to learn. Darlings, if you only knew.

The next summer I accepted an invitation for a holiday in Yugoslavia. I had already met Vera Maletic and her mother in Zagreb in their handsome apartment and Laban-based dance school. The Yugoslavian regime was communist under the tyrant President Tito. Vera's father being one of his victims had been demoted from a significant figure to nightwatchman. The family kept a low profile. In summer 1959 they invited me to join their annual holiday on the island of Lopud. I met them in Dubrovnic where we took a boat across the Adriatic to a dilapidated villa, our home for four weeks. Other guests included the Brabants sisters, well-known dancers from Belgium, Lisa Ullmann, the family maid and Vera's brother Sasha. I had no idea Lisa would be there. There was no love between us but poor soul she was in deep mourning, facing a future alone.

With consternation I discovered that nudity was the form. In the shade of a grove of olives we disrobed and lay basking, reading, dropping down into the clear blue sea to swim with fish, sea urchins and crabs. Here we stayed all day until as the heat of the day ebbed we repaired to the villa for dinner. There the flies were tormenting, the drainage indescribable, but the company, conversation, artistic discourse, food were *formidable*. Sasha was an attraction, a dark, handsome, medical student, but I was in no mood to facilitate his plans for a holiday affair which one has to say were exacerbated by the easy access to naked sunbathing flesh.

Unfortunately the drains did their worst and I contracted infectious hepatitis. With a hundred-day incubation I knew nothing of it until November when I succumbed to intolerable pains in my joints, a rash and sickness. Rushed into St Mary Abbot's hospital in South Kensington I gradually turned a ghastly yellow so the truth dawned. My liver capitulated. I lost two stone, living on a diet of fruit, especially lychees, brought in by the faithful Margaret.

The hospital had been a workhouse, my ward was number two of four, adjoining, Ward 1 for acute, mostly young patients with dire illnesses, exuding cries of distress; Ward 2, mine, acute but expected to live, mostly; Ward 3 over 60s, chronic, with doubtful life expectancy; Ward 4 over 70s who died regularly, their bodies being carted through our ward cleverly disguised under folded blankets. Other living creatures were cockroaches, hundreds of them, who drowned in my lemonade on their nightly invasions. Once a week the wards were fumigated but it was a vain attempt at mass murder.

I recall five people who passed through my ward during my four-month stay. On my left was Violet, rigid with rheumatoid arthritis. She accepted to be a guinea pig and was put on an experimental regime. One morning she sat up and hooted with delight, sang and shouted for she was able to move. It was the first trial of diclofenic and it worked, the side effects that would eventually surface remaining to be seen. For now she soared.

Opposite me was a friend of the poet Robert Frost, his secretary I believe, a quiet woman, erudite, visited from time to time by this man who they said was Frost. I was so ill-educated I had never heard of Robert Frost or his 'road less travelled'.

In the corner bed was a youngish thin woman who wandered up and down pausing at the large windows inhaling the foggy London air. She had lung cancer and I witnessed, or heard, her death for it was not quiet. The nurses tried to help her but she died of gradual asphyxiation and it was unbearable to hear her struggles. Next to her was a madam of a lorry drivers' café who had obviously served her men well or her girls had, for the lads came in unhappy groups, cheering her up, wondering when their solace would return and *Mum*, as they called her, would reopen.

One night the ambulance crew brought in a large plastic sling holding a woman of uncertain age or race, it was impossible to tell. All I could see at first were her feet, black with grime, then emaciated legs covered in sores. She was in a pitiable state, found apparently abandoned in a knacker's yard. By morning she had died, poor thing.

London being multicultural the rituals of death enacted at St Mary Abbotts were various and fascinating to me as I lay in my yellow stupor. Groups of distressed mourners passed through Ward 2, some in quiet solemnity uttering in unison as they went, others wailing in huddles, veiled and gesticulating. I could not help wondering how my passage through the ward might be if I died, for on one occasion my mother visited me and held my hand beseeching me to hold on. So it is that bad, is it, I thought. Not really encouraging.

Eventually I recovered enough to be discharged, unable to stand, let alone to look after myself. I lost 152 Earls Court Road and was driven to my long-suffering mother to recuperate. Still a skeletal figure I gradually gained weight and strength. This sorry tale did, however, have a happy ending for after a while I went to live with Elizabeth, now married to Jim, in Sevenoaks, and I was eventually well enough to dance again and return to teaching at Dartford.

Sevenoaks being an artistic town, amateur music and drama thrived. Among the backstage crew was a quiet young man, John Dunlop, but that will have to lead to another chapter.

Letter from Laban on the notation book he was planning

Above Marion North, Ico the cat and me in the Art of Movement Studio's new home in Weybridge, the beginning of a long professional relationship

Below Dancers at Dartford College of Physical Education

Above left Using an icosahedron to demonstrate at Dartford College of Physical Education

Above right William Elmhirst with Laban in the garden of the Art of Movement Studio

Left Sheer vitality and creativity of the Dartford dancers

Demonstrating at a Ling PE Conference with two Dartford students

CHAPTER 11

1961

John

Last year I gave what were probably my last workshops, my body suggests. Invited by Bedford University to contribute to their professional development course, I stayed a night with Tina, and another with Rosalind, Margaret Rosewarne's daughters. The two women could not be more different, Tina, mother of two, a professional woman who has never been without full-time employment, Rosalind, a dynamic entrepreneur, passionate about plants, leading a more hazardous self-employed way of life. They have been friends of my children from the beginning when we all went on seaside holidays together over forty years ago.

My mind turned to 152 Earls Court Road where one day, after a gruelling afternoon contrasting Maslow's and Piaget's theories of needs and learning, Margaret and I had stopped for a whisky and soda and agreed that if we were to marry anyone we had better get on with it, she being thirty-six and I twenty-nine. She did first within the year, to Donald, a fellow sports person, and I followed suit, to John.

In Sevenoaks, while still recovering my health from hepatitis, John Dunlop and I passed each other during the rehearsals for Britten's *Noye's Fludde*. He made the ark and I played percussion and choreographed the solos for the Dove and the Raven. Then it was *Dido and Aeneas*, with my sister on continuo, then Gilbert and Sullivan. John sang tenor in the chorus and I played drum kit in the orchestra pit. One evening for a performance of *The Yeoman of the Guard*, a four-inch high Beefeater was to be found on my bass drum. I placed it aside and played the overture. What is this? I had a good look at the Yeoman on their first chorus to see who might look my way. And John did.

Some months later, with Cupid lurking, we relaxed in a local public bar. Over a beer, our conversation was mathematical, concerning parallel lines that appear ultimately to merge. Next morning John went on holiday and I realised that actually he had proposed.

A fortnight later I met him at Charing Cross. We made for St James Park and there surrounding by ducks and tourists he knelt. 'Be my wife,' he said. Oh my God, I thought, this is it.

We went to *The Times* to announce our engagement and on to Gorringes to buy a beautiful sapphire ring, which I am wearing as I type. The students at Dartford disrupted their examination schedule as they passed on the news. Firstly, as *The Times* revealed, I was the daughter of a bishop, was it possible? Secondly, John's father, Sir John Dunlop was a well-known diplomat, truly? To celebrate, John and I bought a sports car and my next teaching day was a riot.

We married and set up home in Sevenoaks and I began to learn who John was. Ours was not a conventional love story, not at all, but a meeting of minds. Although John was relatively wealthy he was not your usual establishment material, not the typical Sennockian tennis, golf, bridge player, praise be. Genuinely his own man, he suffered from having a father with a huge personality and an international career that made him expect to be heard. John's mother had been a sad figure, postnatal depression having crushed her. She had never cared for or loved her son or made a home for him. While her husband progressed abroad from brigadier to consul general she had taken her own life while John was at Cambridge. 'Was that awful,' I asked. 'No, I didn't know her,' he said. I thought of my mother who had done anything and everything for us girls as far as her imagination, her strength and her penury could achieve.

While Sir John, now retired, put himself about, very ably, in Sevenoaks overshadowing his quieter son, little did the Sennockians know the truth for John owned the substantial Dunlop family house allowing his father to live there as he had no wish that we should live in his unhappy childhood home. John gave his father an allowance to enable him to continue his façade and never said a word, never let on. John just waited patiently for us, together, to find a project of our own.

Intellectually John was brilliant with a memory to die for, a natural linguist. In his day job he used those skills as an international patent attorney. As a member of the local pub quiz team he was unsurpassable. The two of us could not have been more different in interests, in capacities, and yet we made a formidable pair for creating new things and stayed together through good times and bad for nigh on fifty years, literally 'till death do you part'.

I continued to teach dance and two years into our married life *A Handbook for Modern Educational Dance* was published and sold thousands. I was deluged with requests to teach courses. The irony was not lost on me. Here was a book dubbed 'the Bible' in which I interpreted Rudolf Laban's radical but impracticably expressed ideas in a down to earth way for teachers of dance of Primary and Secondary children when I myself had never done it. What I had seen were students struggling with no practical book to refer to so had written one directly with them and their like in mind. The book is, as I write, still in print, in several languages.

I resigned from Dartford and instead gave guest workshops all over the country. John knew that marriage for me did not mean full-time wifehood, which was still the common practice in the 1960s. That was understood from the start. While we were engaged the contract for *A Handbook* had been achieved and we had celebrated in a pub by Charing Cross station, me already inebriated, for John Macdonald of Macdonald and Evans, publisher, liked to ply gin and tonic to his young authors, to test their head for liquor. I obviously passed muster.

Being interested in the problems that arise from dance as an ephemeral art, disappearing as you whirl and step and fall and rise, when Lisa Ullmann proposed an international forum for dance notation I joined immediately and before long was its chairperson. Combative debates took place between participants who came from two worlds. The Americans had developed Labanotation with a professional dance purpose to record and copyright choreographic theatre works, while the Europeans, especially folk dance specialists, had a research purpose. They kept the system's original more academically suitable name Kinetography Laban. Inevitably trouble brewed.

How you use your torso as a Martha Graham dancer or a Balanchine dancer is precise, distinct, and requires detailed analysis and notation. A Magyar szardas or a Yemeni hopla, primarily step dances, let the dancer's torso have a more free rein, less analysis, fewer signs and symbols. No wonder the ground rules of the grammar of the notation shook somewhat. Having worked with both American Ann Hutchinson and European Albrecht Knust I separated the stars and stripes tornado from the Prussian brick wall, daily. The first of these spats took place in 1961, a few months before our wedding so John in a spirit of support attended parts of the conference as a way of getting a glimpse at what took my interest.

We agreed for fun that he would study for the elementary examination in dance notation which he passed, and I would study for the elementary patent exam. Let me tell you that writing a patent specification for an innovative pair of scissors with only words as tools, no diagrams and no gesturing, was tough. I failed.

During the second international notation conference the Berlin Wall, dividing communist east from capitalist west, went up. A dilemma confronted those participants who lived on the Russian side of the wall. To go home immediately or to stay in the west; whichever way, how? Ingeborg Beier, the notator at Unter den Linden Opera House in Berlin, went back. She was clearly terrified at the thought but fled.

A year later John and I were in West Berlin at an international patent gathering held there surely as a western political statement for at that time Berlin was in the Russian zone of occupation with West Berlin a British pocket surrounded by a hostile communist siege. West Berlin was kept going through an airlift of all supplies, food, everything. Into that wasp's nest we flew to a military airfield.

The situation was bizarre. The conference ended with a formal ball held in the Radio Centre. As a new wife to these events I was gathered up by a patriarchal Swede in white tie and tails, I in new ball gown with elbow length white gloves. We waltzed and slow fox-trotted elegantly in sight of The Wall on the other side of which was Ingeborg Beier in poverty and in fear.

John and I determined to go across and make sure she was managing. Checkpoint Charlie is a tourist attraction now but then, new, it terrified. Separated from John I was photographed, my passport taken away, all my money and anything worth anything removed. One had to change £100 into East German currency and spend it while there. Sent across a long no-man's-land alley with a Russian rifle pointing at me I waited for John on the other side unnerved in a way I had never experienced before.

We held hands and walked by the war-scarred, barbed-wired Brandenburg Gate aware that we were being watched as we entered the Opera House. The only bit of it that appeared to be working was a café in the cavernous basement. It reminded me of the Red Cross food centres during the war, plain in every respect with sparse and barely edible food. We saw Ingeborg and she saw us but she made no move to meet us.

Eventually by subtle body movement she indicated, 'Go,' clearly terrified to be seen with a westerner and of course we stood out.

Over the years I made several visits to East Berlin when writing Laban's biography, travelling by train through the passport check to Alexander Platz, scared but determined. My first aim was to locate Ilse Loesch, a woman who had worked with him in the 1920s and 30s. Having shared his egalitarian views she went further and had embraced Communism. As a valued Party member she was allotted a 'flat', one room, concrete throughout. Our conversation was informative of the past but guarded of the present. It was impossible to know what she thought or knew or felt. I didn't ask, just concentrated on her pre-war experiences with Laban.

I was reminded of my first visit to Moscow with John on one of his international patent events. As the attorneys communed on the niceties of the law on invention in Russia I was allotted a 'carer', a severe woman who shepherded me to those parts of the city deemed right for the foreigner to see. After a morning looking at an aircraft museum and a glove factory I had suggested hopefully that a contemporary art exhibition might be of interest. She complied and I found myself in a room in which sat rows of the populace bussed in for cultural duties, staring at art works with no interest whatever.

On the third day my carer was becoming desperate to find me suitable visits. I suggested the Lenin Library and she deemed it permissible. I knew the originals of the Stepanov dance notation system were housed there, the system adapted by Vaslav Nijinsky to record his famous *The Rite of Spring* dances. The name Stepanov turned out to be somewhat like Smith or Jones with scores of entries so I searched for his first name, Vladimir. Unfamiliar with Russian handwriting I missed that V and B are interchangeable. Eventually I found владимир Stepanov and the papers were brought up to me.

That library visit was more successful than breakfast which consisted of a plate of plain yoghurt with anchovies on the side gulped down with a spoonful of the strongest acorn coffee ever. I bemused the waitress by asking for a larger cup of coffee, having a *café au lait* in mind. She complied bringing me a monster cup in the bottom of which lay the same spoonful of black acorn liquid. Ah well.

As a reminder of the visit John and I bought a splendid coffee pot with six monster cups. I drink from one every Saturday morning with a *latte* as, in a leisurely manner, I read *The Times*.

Original (pink) cover, somewhat dog-eared after 53 years, of my first book *A Handbook for Modern Educational Dance*

John Henderson Dunlop

John and me and our wedding cake, with an icosahedron as decoration

Albrecht Knust demonstrating at an ICKL Conference, me as Chairperson
behind him, with Jacqueline Challet Haas (France), Diana Baddeley
(Germany), Lucy Venables (USA), Ann Hutchinson (USA), Roderyk Lange
(Poland), Maria Szentpal (Hungary), Mina Jonsdottir (Iceland), Vivien Bridson
(GB), Emma Lugossy (Hungary), and 2 others. (Ph. Willy van Heekern,
Fotoarchiv Ruhr Museum)

Looking at the 'Lunohod 1' moon exploration craft in the Space Museum in
Moscow

CHAPTER 12

1964

Beechmont and Co Unlimited

In the third year of our marriage the possibility of a joint project emerged. I think of that moment every time I put on my gardening boots. Heaving bags of compost is not a job for an octogenarian but I do it in my Blackheath veg patch, with an aching body and a singing heart. I am inordinately proud of it, I love it. Somehow being close to mother earth makes my soul fly, urging seeds to germinate, cuttings to root, and fruit to ripen, planting beans and courgettes with tender loving care. Last week I completed the winter pruning, the gooseberry, blackcurrant, autumn raspberries and tayberry and with arthritic hands and unsteady legs I did it. Will this year be the last? Maybe.

My veg patch is five large strides by six larger strides, give or take a shoe's length. Beechmont, on the other hand, was sixteen acres and whoever did the mowing took a five mile hike. Beechmont's rebirth came about because one night I could not sleep and turning over towards my slumbering fairly new spouse, whispered my vision. 'Why don't we buy Beechmont?'

Beechmont was a derelict Victorian estate, just over the road from our modest Sevenoaks home. Destroyed in 1944 by a doodlebug while occupied by the army, the ruins, the drives, the terraces, the orangery and greenhouses, the ballroom, smoking room, classic upstairs downstairs ménage, had vanished. Layers of brambles and self-sewn elders smothered the ruins. Nature had taken over. We knew it as a wild place for a walk or a picnic.

For better for worse we bought it with no planning permission. I don't need to say that all our family and friends said, 'You're mad.' We agreed, and set about turning our madness into a dream and a reality. Come rain or snow, John and I laboured to find what was there. Hours, days, weekends, evenings we pulled and sawed and chopped and bonfired to reveal a wondrous possibility of views over the Weald of Kent. Hidden were a wealth of noble conifers and rhododendron arbours, bluebell woods and wild orchids, with fox and badger lairs.

It is difficult to communicate the extent of our endeavour over two years. Planning permission was given to replace the mansion or rather to build our new house touching the old drawing room, to build my dance studio complex in place of the ballroom and a cottage for helpers where once stood the dairies and stables. The architect said, 'You're mad.' We agreed and hired him.

On a practical level the army occupation and destruction had a positive side for we found a pristine drainage system, never used, by falling into twenty-four leaf-filled manholes. We discovered three terraces on the south side and set about designing a rose garden, a wild rose bank and a fruit garden. On the east we uncovered steps to a long formal walkway and below it a derelict orangery that we transformed into a swimming pool terrace. Rhododendrons that had been smothered by elders started to bloom, the muddy track from the road transformed into a broad driveway, the bluebells flowered again and the walkways in the woods became passable.

Using the words 'discovered' and 'uncovered' does not describe what we did at all. With weed trees everywhere, chest-high stinging nettles, all-embracing brambles, wasps' nests and adders, we were explorers, labourers, tractor drivers, tree fellers. We were scratched, stung, soaked through but ever persisting.

Despite the wider family's bewilderment they rallied, Sir John bestowing his blessing without actually doing anything. My sister Robina grafted two hundred roses from her stock to start off our rose garden and her teenage young donned wellies and took secateurs, saws and hatchets to break paths through the wilderness and help John and I make a heaven on earth, which we did.

Horticulturally the site gave technical interest for it lay on the Green Sand Ridge. I learnt that green sand soil is acid and ideal for azaleas, rhododendrons and heathers and set about learning the difference between davidii and hortensii, erica and calluna, Japanese, dwarf, spreading, grafted and recumbent. The soil where the mansion had stood was quite different, alkaline from the mortar, so I set about choosing shrubs and trees that would tolerate lime and flourish there, amelanchia, double may, crab apples, flowering currants. I learned their species, their height, their root run, their bark colour. I instructed the gardener where, how, with what fertilizer to plant them all as if I had been trained at Wisley, when in fact my fingers were crossed. But flourish they did.

Daily John commuted to his office in Chancery Lane to pursue patents and I somehow wrote textbooks and led courses hither and yon. The contractors arrived on site to start the three buildings, John taking charge of the siting of each and their architectural dimensions while I designed the colours and textures, woods, tiles, carpets and so on. Around it all we continued our horticultural endeavours and by summer of 1967 we moved in.

It was a crazy few years made complicated by the studio being completed first and the Ministry of Education inviting me to lead courses there in the early attempts to put in place the first university degrees in dance. But we were young and strong and with a vision and felt invincible.

We moved into the new house, unfinished, surrounded by a chaotic sixteen acre half-made garden and a working dance studio. There we celebrated our son Roger's second birthday with the builders and their children together with Roger's looker-after, a robust and loud lady with a three-year-old daughter. Simultaneously each evening John and I were performing in a Gilbert and Sullivan opera while during the day I had a group of college lecturers in for a two-week course in the studio during which I gave a seminar at Essex University to their research group that tested my intellectual wits to their limit. Pressure on all sides. Anyone with sense would have realised that all that was too much for a mere human and my head decided just that and collapsed.

It is a strange experience to have a mental breakdown, and breakdown it was, starting with a vicious fever and loss of speech. Something had snapped. I could not bear sound or sight. For some reason red was anathema even if pale pink. Suffice it to say I was whisked off to peace and quiet for some months and returned still in a very delicate state. It was more than a year before I could write my name. I imagined, in the manic moments when I had to shut the world out, that a visor enveloped me, for that is what it felt like, a metal curtain descending over my head between me and reality. How lucky I was that everyone rallied.

Life went on around me while I remained unable to take responsibility for myself or anything else. In those days treatments for mental illness were in their infancy. Clearly I did not need emotional counselling or psychotherapy. I was put onto a trial drug that lowered sensation so that sound and sight became somewhat bearable again, slowly.

Throughout, my assistant for Beechmont Movement Study Centre, Paddy Macmaster, an ex-Dartford dance student, capable and willing, kept the professional work going. Together we had written the first four *Readers in Motif Writing*, (my adaptation of Laban's notation to accommodate improvisation and creativity). The texts pleased the Inspectors of Education who thought a notation for dance might push the academic hierarchy to see that dance was degree worthy, literacy being an accessible concept to them. And the academics did.

At this point Lisa Ullmann, unnecessarily nervous that what I was putting in place might undermine her institution, attempted to close down Beechmont Movement Study Centre through sending me a solicitor's letter demanding that I cease trading quoting a law of restraint of competition within a fifty-mile radius of her Art of Movement Studio. My way of dealing with her threat was to ignore it but it did not sweeten our relationship. The capable Paddy continued to teach the dancers on her own, taking out our courses on the new notation method to colleges all over the country, while I remained incapacitated.

The life of Beechmont began to take shape around me. The estate was developing as an Eden with each season providing beauty, each day producing new discoveries, new vistas, new foxholes. Looking at the notes I made for the gardener some eight years into the Beechmont adventure I see I advised him on feeding the rose garden, clipping the heather bed, watering the new azaleas, cleaning the pond in the wellington bed, pruning the rugosa hedge, mowing the circular lawn, planting an amelanchia, checking the heater of the swimming pool, edging the drive, sharpening the saw and filling up the tractor. Sometimes as I sit alone in Blackheath in the fading light looking out over the grassy triangle of Lock Chase I sip a chilled glass of Croft Original, a favourite aperitif sherry of ours and dream of those first years at Beechmont.

Many a summer evening on John's return from a day's work in Chancery Lane we sat on Beechmont's blue slate patio as the lights of Kent, one by one, emerged. We were well aware that we lived a life of privilege, no worries of mortgage or jobs or bills or debts.

We would consider the progress of our son, a child of intense energy. Roger took to his bath at 6pm exhausted with his day's adventures and ready for bed. Above us in the children's wing, keeping an eye on his sleeping head, sat a Swiss au pair girl, living as a family friend. John shared with me the inventions that he had patented that day, the wondrously simple drop of oil in a ballpoint pen of Mr Biro, the complex life-saving visor of Concorde, the supersonic airliner. I shared with him the progress of the peonies and the new weeping pear and, as I slowly recovered my wits, the progress of my latest book.

John being the generous sweet man he was, wanted to share everything Beechmont offered with other people and I suppose my childhood education from my parents complied. We started with the swimming pool. Families could join for a modest fee, children came for swimming lessons. Being on the bottom terrace families could get in via a side gate and we might hear laughter and shrieks of fun in the distance. The paddling pool was just right for the little ones and the main pool for adventure.

Then the studio was used for all manner of socialising when not full of dancers. The Sevenoaks Music Club met there, the two grand pianos being an attraction. The Youth Orchestra made the studio their home, clubs hired the place for evening events, professionally dancers came for week-long courses. With a sprung floor and full-length windows we flew and whirled and made art with the Inspectors of Education popping in from time to time. What a turn around for me from cold Oxford Road and grubby Westbourne Grove.

When my second child was on the way I attempted to retire professionally for having collapsed in Roger's youth, I embraced discretion over valour. I had learnt that one can't do everything. The only way emotionally I could 'retire' was to put all my dance books in the cellar so that nothing reminded me of the thing to which I was umbilically attached.

A year or so later Margaret Thatcher denied that 'society' existed and demanded that everyone look after themselves, or some such antisocial dictate. The Archbishop of Canterbury's response was to set community centre stage in the parishes of the United Kingdom with I suppose the parable of the Good Samaritan in mind. 'Work out what this will mean for you,' he wrote. He struck a chord with me and before long I had started a club for disadvantaged people, people with disasters in their lives, loss of limb, blindness, stroke victims. They appeared out of nowhere, previously hidden from sight. Willing residents in the vicinity joined in to work on a rota, to cook and supervise a purposeful day, Brattlewood residents one week, The Rise a second, White Hart Wood a third, with their retired husbands providing the transport.

Before long we had a Monday Club for men and women with disasters, a Wednesday Club for people with learning difficulties, a Thursday Club with the Monday Club's overflow, the Saturday PHAB Club for able-bodied and physical handicapped young people, a Sunday Club for older people living alone. The rule of play was that no difference was made between club member and helper. All helped all. A deaf person would fill in the welfare forms for a blind person, people would exchange recipes, thread each others' needles, hold others' wool skeins, guide each other round the garden, sing together, even dance.

One member, Brian, thirty, angry and disagreeable, had lost his legs in a train accident. One day I wheeled him down to the pool and said, 'Get in.' 'I can't swim,' he said. 'I know', I said and pushed him in jumping in alongside. I had not reckoned that with the weight of his legs not there his head would sink and his rear would rise. Diving under him I managed to get him afloat as it were on top of me. Brian learnt to swim, ceased to see himself as disadvantaged, joined a swimming club and trained competitively. When the Paralympics started he was there. Hooray. But what would Health and Safety have had to say?

Sometimes it was the progress of our daughter that John and I considered over sherry, a redhead of thoughtful observation who stayed alert until 11pm. In our family there were few rules, but enforced. 'Tell me when you go off the property. Never go to the swimming pool alone. Appear when the gong rings for meals. After 8pm is grown-up time.' Emma would appear, at 8.15, a small pyjama-ed person sitting on the bottom stair, hoping to be invited in to the adults-only space. In due time, she always was, and curling up on the hearthrug she listened as John and I discussed the plans for the new heather garden, the miners' strike, John's next trip abroad, the need for a second gardener, or the next Music Club's concert in the studio. No wonder Emma grew up to be mature in mind before her years.

The clubs became part of our family life. As soon as Emma could crawl she was inducted. My mother, by now blind and living with us, attended as a club member and made firm friends with Mrs Culver our retired gardener's widow. The clubs lasted for twenty-five years, long after I had returned to dance and long after I had passed on the leadership to others. As an experiment in community it certainly worked, so shame on you Margaret Thatcher.

The other day, forty-five years after the birth of the clubs I discovered that one of them is still alive and well, and called The Beechmont Club. Next week a charity leader concerned with community inclusion is coming to interview me on how we got started and maintained such a mutually beneficial endeavour. Could a similar thing be successful in today's technological celebrity culture?

With no dance, music became important to me. I learned tympani and tuned percussion and played in the Sevenoaks Orchestra and the Tonbridge Philharmonic, both quality amateur orchestras whose players were lawyers, doctors, students, mothers, dentists by day but who brought their expertise together to make music for the local community. I gave my best to bass drum in the Dies Irae of Verdi's *Requiem*, the castanets in *El Salon Mexico*, the tympani in the storm of Beethoven's *Pastoral Symphony*, metal sticks on an anvil for *Balshazzar's Feast* and sleigh bells for a Christmas Special.

One musical event stands out for me as a player, Kurt Weill's chamber opera *Down in the Valley*. Scored for a plethora of percussion instruments, two of us rehearsed long and hard, both Trevor (a doctor) and I tested to the limit. It was the layout of beaters and complex quick changes from one instrument to another that had us concentrating, counting, dodging across each other, watching for cues. Playing for Britten's community opera *Noye's Fludde* had been easy compared with this. In *Noye* the percussionist's task includes sorting out the cups for the raindrops that introduce the flood. Their theme is played on tuned cups hanging from an old-fashioned towel horse. Finding the right cups to ting the raindrop scale took patience and denuded my kitchen.

The Tunbridge Wells Philharmonic was perhaps a cut above both the Sevenoaks and Tonbridge orchestras, with more ambitious concerts. I once sang as an alto with their choir in Rutter's *Magnificat*, with its soaring treble solo. One concert there remains vivid to this day and I was neither playing nor singing, Haydn's *Creation*, not normally a work I would choose, being a 20th century devotee myself. But Emma, by then a professional singer, was engaged as soloist, not her regular *métier* which was consort singing, one-voice-to-a-part. Here she sang the soprano roles of both the archangel Gabriel and Eve in Act Two.

Emma is not tall, she stood, a lone little figure in the gaping black box and from her mouth issued forth a bell-like sound, vibrant and expressive. I was looking forward to the concert but hadn't expected my response. I shuddered throughout my entire body, I all but cried out, I was overwhelmed, struck in the gut by the beauty and simplicity of her voice.

My mother with her granddaughter Emma

Above John clearing Beechmont in all weathers

Below left Me clearing Beechmont in all weathers

Below right My Blackheath veg patch

Paddy Macmaster teaching with the new notation in the Beechmont
Movement Study Centre studio

Tuning up for a rehearsal in the studio with Sevenoaks Orchestra

Instructing three college lecturers in the writing of dance notation scores

John and me on the newly-made top terrace, dressed for a Buckingham Palace garden party

Some of the Monday Club members with collaborator Pat Downing standing

A Monday Club Christmas Party some fifteen years later with the mayor of Sevenoaks

CHAPTER 13

1976

Family Life

The invitation came today for a wedding, Alison's granddaughter, for sure an occasion for a gathering of the Preston clan and an inevitable occasion for anno domini to interject that we are not immortal. Alison, now over 90, will be there held together by her carer. Elizabeth will be there, if I bring her, hopefully steady on her battered pins, and me the third sister, failing but not yet failed.

Not so many years ago John and Dorothy, a significant person in my professional life, and I holidayed, and the morning ritual included John putting on his hearing aid, Dorothy her foot brace, and I my denture before we gathered for a civilised breakfast. Ah well, age will out. For us three Preston girls the count today is equally specific for Alison needs her clock, by which she retains her grip on the world, by organising every five minutes throughout the day, precisely, rigidly. For Elizabeth, two hearing aids to aid her social whirl, for me, a timer to alert me to stop doing what I am doing in time for the next. We three will all be there dressed and hatted for the occasion, Alison stoic in blue, Elizabeth in pink with a feathery 'fascinator' and I with a scarlet pillbox perched over black velvet trouser suit. We will do the young couple proud, each in her own way.

Small people featured throughout the celebrations, on all fours and vertical, in variety, taking me back to the rumbustious days of my children's childhood. Roger was on his feet by ten months, never still or in one place for more than a blink, full of ideas, full of adventure, but balanced by a need to stay within range, within sight, with a love of little things, his beloved gerbil, his model railway carefully planned, created, tended, saved-up for. At three he joined his cousin Mary Mary Quite Contrary, four-year-old redhead mobster. Together they created mayhem in 'Scamps College', alias the local nursery school.

Emma, on the other hand, took her time, vertical by fifteen months, observant, fastidious, taking it all in, toys, drawing, stories, music. Hers was a more measured pace, more thought through, an indoor girl but A1 swimmer. At three she joined the playgroup that I started at Beechmont and her leaning towards things conceptual began to emerge. What we did not realise (and how, I ask myself, as a mother could one not realise?) was that Emma's sight was quite severely impaired. She could read at an early age, so impaired sight? Surely not. But she had to concentrate to align her two eyes, then she saw well. Otherwise things were a bit of a blur. I only discovered the truth when I suggested she go into a shop, one that she passed every day in the car on her way to school so she surely knew it. She didn't, she had never seen it, just 'blurred' it.

Realising that one did not know one's own child was deeply shocking and has led me to be anxious that as a working mother I neglected my children. They assure me that when they needed me I was there, always. Perhaps it is because of my own childhood when indeed I hardly knew my mother and relied on first beloved Nanny and then on myself and my older sister Elizabeth as my mother struggled to cope with widowhood and penury.

With Emma's birth I took five years out from professional work, attempted to shift my mind to family life. I qualified in Playgroup Leadership for which I kept a diary of the minutiae of childhood. Emma's conservative taste in food, noted on my chart, came to a crisis point in France. We were camped in a caravan near Amiens, Roger exploring the village, tentatively, but Emma was confounded by the fact that she could not understand the people. 'They can't speak,' she declared. Of course sound was more important to her than sight. Not one ounce of French food would she eat, would she even try. Eventually in desperation on day three she agreed to try a crêpe.

One rainy day we went to the local cinema. Roger enjoyed the action while Emma asked throughout the hour and a half, 'What are they saying?' Of course, she couldn't see the action, could she? Back home, eye specialists being available, her impairment was dealt with but I was more observant of my children after that, or tried to be.

My sight is deteriorating unquestionably despite injections in the eye. As I sit in my battered armchair, on which I wrote my first book in Earls Court Road, I reach for Nancy's magnifying glass, used by her until her sight diminished totally. John and I made a home for her while Emma was a small person. Her bed became a repository for George the cat and Emma, both held spellbound by Nancy's warmth and storytelling. I had forgotten, but yesterday, calling in on Emma's domain, she brought out a notebook, made collectively in that bedroom, Nancy's own childhood, typed and roughly sketched by me and crayoned by Emma's young fingers. I hope I have the guts to do what Nancy did, just say one day, 'I am going to a nursing home, before I become a nuisance.'

John was a natural father, perhaps because he had missed out on his own childhood. He loved books and read aloud with dramatic impersonations of Tigger (*zforzando*), Roo (*pianissimo*), Owl (*grave in the minor key*) Kanga (*cantabile*). A visit to the Wild Wood, alias Ashdown Forest, made a perfect day out for all with Roger holding his own Pooh Bear firmly by the hand throughout. Of the Peter Rabbit books Jemima Puddle-Duck was a favourite, John giving the wily fox the voice of a popular film gangster. Emma vouchsafed that Jemima was a very silly bird and we all agreed.

Years later cousin Mary Mary concocted a wondrous costume for Jemima while working in the wardrobe department of the Royal Opera House for the first production for the Royal Ballet's *Tales of Beatrix Potter*. It must have been one of the last of Frederick Ashton's choreographies. I could not help thinking of his patent leather shoes passing the head-high window of the basement workshop in Knightsbridge's Yeoman's Row, where in 1952 Nan Austin and I clad Festival Ballet for their opening season at the Festival Hall.

John had a passion for fireworks and November 5th at Beechmont was noisy. When the children were young John prepared a display on the climbing frame and small friends gathered with sparklers in their fists, to ooh and ah. A bit later, teenage years, we combined November 5th with Hallowe'en dressing up as skeletons and all manner of ghoulies and ghosties ending with a huge bonfire in the garden. The house offered fruitful opportunities for youthful Hallowe'en pranks. We set up a ghost 'train', Emma's timorous friends urged up the back stairs to take courage and walk through the totally dark corridor where Roger's friends lay in wait in the hidden doorways to waylay the girls with all things frightening. It was so wonderfully scary they rushed round to do it again and again.

John's international patenting enabled us to travel, to wherever innovation was. Once to the Venetian island of Murano to watch the master glassblowers make their wares. Every morning I look at the vase I was given there as a thank you for John's labours, its golden flecks in rose coloured stipple, its arching shape, a wondrous object. We visited Basle, Swiss Aluminium, standing in awe peering into the vats of liquid metal at temperatures too hot to measure heated by electric cable six inches thick.

On we flew to Chicago, John to discuss new patents with the president of Illinois Tool Works while his wife entertained me in their shopping mall's restaurant shaped like a boat. Every half hour we moved rhythmically, dipping and diving as at sea, which with a serving of oysters was a disconcerting experience. On to Ohio on legal business, where I dropped into the University Dance Department.

Was that the biggest mistake of my life or the inevitable beginning of what had to be for I knew from that moment that I had to return to dance. My body whispered Yes, my head screamed No, for I foresaw immediately the issues it would raise, problems for all of us. How could one believe that a woman with all that I had at Beechmont could think that dance, useless, valueless dance, could be such a magnet? But it was.

On we went to San Francisco for an international patent gathering, where I took on the role of a supportive wife of a partner of Gill Jennings and Every. The two other partner's wives were English roses, gowned demurely and handsomely, while I was in an all-in-one trouser suit and flowing coat that John loved, but clearly not the wear for a firm prizing its conservative reliability. Ah well.

We returned home, beautiful home, but the glimpse of dance at Ohio made me restless and before the year was out, with the children in school, I decided to go back to school myself. I knew I could not return to professional work without some qualifications for I had none and dance, now in academia, had moved on. Marion North, my erstwhile colleague from days at Weybridge, now Principal of the Laban Centre for Movement and Dance, plotted a way to get me accepted on an advanced course of study, provided I would teach at the same time. I agreed.

So began a time of double life, children, Beechmont, John, clubs, music, five years from which I gained a postgraduate Diploma, a Masters degree and a Doctorate.

Mother and son,
me with Roger

Emma in
thoughtful mood

John and me with tractor, children and the dog, working in the gardens at Beechmont

Roger and Emma admiring Angelika the au pair, with Stephen and Beverley the gardener's children, enjoying the freedom of Beechmont's acres

CHAPTER 14

1977

Conflict of Interest

Summer 1977 was a year to remember where family and professional work crunched. It started joyously with the whole clan assembled at Long Ashton church for the wedding of Robina Ann, the eldest of Nancy's twelve grandchildren, Emma being the youngest by almost thirty years. I had been invited to Ohio State University Dance Department, to guest teach on their summer school, my first work assignment abroad.

As the wedding reception got into full swing I slipped away to Heathrow. All went well for a few days as I introduced the principles of perception to the dancers, using the new knowledge I was acquiring in my studies, giving them fresh ways of looking at dance and seeing what was actually there. But a phone call from John told me that Nancy was in a critical state, was dying.

Oh God, what now? To ignore my mother or give up on the Ohio dancers? I abandoned the dancers, took the first flight home to find home in chaos. Roger had smashed his hand in his go-cart, Emma had broken her leg at school and Nancy lay in a coma.

Nancy's was the first dying that I experienced close to. The carer at her nursing home would not let me into her bedside. 'She is trying to go. If she hears you she will think you need her. She will try to come back. Please let her go.' I had never thought that one might try to die as a voluntary act. Then I realised that she had been waiting for Robina Ann to marry, for however up to the times Nancy tried to be she was still traditional at heart. To her, marriage was essential for a woman's happiness and now, with Robina Ann settled, she could let herself go.

I was unprepared for my response, I was utterly disoriented by her death. After all I had been independent of my mother since childhood, hadn't I? I cared for her partly, I had told myself, out of duty. What rot, what rubbish, for the first time in my life I knew how much I loved her.

As I waited outside her room for her last breath it was as if a veil lifted as I gave her my all, my will that she could go peacefully. I saw her life as a whole as never before, clearly, not clouded by my needs. Her unloved childhood, the appalling death of her first love at Passchendaele, her marriage to my father, her second widowhood on his untimely death, her wondrous coping with the upbringing of her four daughters on a widow's mite. As we lowered her coffin into the grave, I heard myself cry out, a groan of dire loss.

Then off on family holiday, a caravan again so we would all be close together, Emma's leg in plaster, Roger with his hand in a mess, me in confused mourning assembling in my mind the children's needs, the dancers in Ohio I had abandoned, a headstone for Nancy's grave, and John, darling John, holding us all together.

In the top drawer in my study is an ancient video tape, a recording of the work I choreographed at that time. *Fragment for a Family* was cast with two dancers, a man and a woman, and two children, Roger aged twelve and Emma aged six. It plotted exactly the tension I felt in the two-sided life I was leading and I suppose was an attempt to bring them together. If I had been unsuccessful in my bid to return to work, out of my depth and failed, how easy it would have been. I could have abandoned dance and academia and embraced home and family. But I wasn't. I was horribly successful, clearly expected to play a significant role.

I could not believe that in the five years that I had been out of dance someone else had not emerged to take my place but they had not. The issue was the future of the work of Rudolf Laban, wretched, brilliant man, who had left a legacy that was treated by Lisa Ullmann as untouchable Holy Grail but by Marion and I as needing to be critiqued and contexted for today as a central tool for integrating movement theory with the reality of contemporary dance practice.

Laban's heritage consisted in several distinct parts, his own choreographic work that was almost lost and in any case thought to be coloured with the flavour of the Weimar Republic, the twenties and early thirties in Germany, thereby suspect, thought to be highly dramatic with insufficient polish. Another was his educational dance of post-war UK, creative and beautiful in a school but seen by the professional dance community as without a technical basis and, again, of no interest to them, with their grades and syllabi.

Another was his extraordinary analysis of movement as an expressive human power and no one had surpassed or even attempted to come close to his understanding let alone proffered an alternative.

Since the Laban Centre was focusing on dance as a current theatre art form the only part of his work that was obviously useful was his analysis. Forget his choreography, for American Modern Dance was the new flavour. Forget his educational work, for the government's educational policy had shifted from promoting creative movement for boys and girls of all ages (such as I experienced at Downe House) to the study of dance as a technically driven art form, including ballet and Graham technique, not including German Expressionism. Adding to the lack of enthusiasm for Laban's work by some was his notation. Recognised as excellent but thought to be difficult, too intellectual, too heady.

That was the scenario that confronted me when I accepted to teach. Professionally I had to discover for myself the Modern Dance of America for it was over here and here to stay with American Bonnie Bird, in situ at the Laban Centre. Our relationship, with her as co-director, was less than straightforward. She wanted Martha Graham in and Rudolf Laban out and I wanted them both in. If you believe in astrology, which I don't and yet... Bonnie was a bull, a Taurus, who liked to engage horns and do battle while I am a fish, a Piscean, who circumvents obstacles and swims on. This mismatch caused Bonnie distress and confusion for I would not engage but continued my quest to radically sift and present Laban's work. As large photographs of Martha were displayed in the entrance hall somehow, overnight, equally large photographs of Rudolf appeared on the opposite wall...

To mark the centenary of Laban's birth Marion instigated an international conference and somewhat uncomfortable it was. In the 1930s many Laban-trained people had emigrated to America, one of whom was Irmgard Bartenieff, movement therapist, who with Ann Hutchinson had expanded the Dance Notation Bureau and trained a caucus of students to develop Laban's ideas for the USA market. To the conference came copious Americans who seemed to feel that their somewhat theoretical and therapeutic way of treating his work was the accepted way. That did not sit happily with me nor with Marion with our focus on dance as a theatre art. The influx was a total nightmare for the Laban old guard now in their eighties, Sylvia Bodmer who had taught me in Manchester, Lisa Ullmann, Sigurd Leeder who was Kurt Jooss's collaborator. They were unprepared for the apparent, albeit misplaced, takeover. Several discussion situations were set up and I found myself chairing awkward sessions as people came face to face with developments quite alien to their own. To round it off I was asked to edit a text on the deliberations. That became *Dancing and Dance Theory* and was published the following year.

Into this flew Dr Dorothy Madden from Maryland University. Someone said, 'This is Dorothy, she is here to supervise your doctorate.' 'Is she indeed,' I said to myself, having fellow American Bonnie Bird in my mind. 'Then I had better discover what she knows and find out if we have anything in common.'

Dorothy had just retired after an award-winning career at Maryland University chairing the Dance Department, having successfully extricated dance from Physical Education. Now she was wondering where and how to spend the last third of her life hoping that some of it could be in dance and possibly settling in the UK with her amour, an English architect with whom she had spent several summers at his holiday house in France. She spoke immaculate French and crossed the Channel at every opportunity.

Dorothy, I discovered, was a cosmopolitan, while Bonnie remained an expat American. Surprisingly her first serious experience in dance had been in German Expressionism, with a dancer trained by Hanya Holm at the New York Mary Wigman school. Her nearest and dearest in New York were choreographer Doris Humphrey and the musician cum choreography guru Louis Horst, both of interest to me.

With a fabulous education in Vermont, curiosity for knowledge was part of her outlook so we started out with a fundamentally shared endeavour to discover more about dance, human expression, modernity, choreography, she having successfully achieved the first doctorate in dance with performance at New York University rather than a purely cerebral one. We got on immediately, exchanging knowledge and witticisms. With London as her English base, alongside her Martha's Vineyard American home, she became, as it were, mid-Atlantic, one foot on either side of the pond. Before long the foot this side brought her to Beechmont.

With no children of her own 'Dear Darling Dorothy', as my children called her, took to proxy grannyhood like a duck to water. Being a pianist in her youth she could gently encourage Emma's piano practice where a mother's ear was definitely scorned. John loved history and together they researched Dorothy's French forebears, the Giffards, one of whom had been William the Conqueror's standard bearer in 1066. What better excuse for a family outing than to find where the Norman invasion started and visit the spot where Guillaume Giffard followed his master aboard ship, flag flying. Roger's educational progress depended on him falling in love with the teacher, preferably a blonde, but he took to Dorothy's charms despite her brunette rinse.

Dance-wise Dorothy and I could get as embroiled in choreographic concepts as had Margaret Rosewarne and I on educational principles and I needed that. My curiosity as to the core of movement's hidden grammar, what made it meaningful, or sometimes so beautiful it caught one's breath, these were ongoing investigations and all absorbing as my doctorate proceeded, with Dorothy's encouragement and John's forbearance for I must have been a distracted spouse.

As for being a working mother, I fear I was more working than mothering. If anyone says that balancing work and family is straightforward, disbelieve them. Even with an au pair *in situ* it was a tussle, for the head more than the hands. Perhaps because I was at the forefront of all things new at my workplace I could be somewhat single minded, sociology, philosophy, aesthetics et al. One day, driving from Beechmont to work to do battle with the academics a small voice said, 'Mum, are you dropping me at school?'

We were half way to London...

My fortieth birthday photograph

Rehearsing the dancers for *Four and One*, my first piece trying out American Modern Dance forms

Bonnie Bird with Merce Cunningham at the Laban Centre (Ph. Peter Sayers)

Dorothy Madden at Beechmont

Dorothy Madden teaching technique at Dartington Hall 1962 (Courtesy Dartington Hall Archive)

Image capture from a rehearsal film of the dramatic ending to *Fragment for a Family*, with Emma, Roger and Raymond Holland

Sigurd Leeder speaking at the Laban Centenary Conference, Sylvia Bodmer and Lisa Ullmann exhausted with Irmgard Bartenieff seated and me hovering. (Ph. Peter Sayers)

CHAPTER 15

1983

Together and Apart

Being married to a patent attorney entailed travel as John's clients were widespread, the patent world itself being international as well as multilayered. John's speciality was inventions in mechanical engineering, machine parts, aircraft, others in his firm covered new ideas in pharmaceuticals, or computing, some were responsible for trademarks and advertising. Keeping up to date was crucial so global networking was a way of life.

That took us to Buenos Aires in 1980 and it was not a comfortable place to be for Argentina was in the midst of a military dictatorship with people 'disappearing' without trace in quite large numbers. The first thing I noticed was the lack of pop music as a daily backdrop. We were so used to the top ten blaring out, to pop idols and pop songs and to a free and easy atmosphere in the streets. Not in Buenos Aires, which exuded an unnerving aura of constraint. The military dominance would erupt a few years later with the Falklands War but for now John and I stuck together and were not unhappy to find an expat community.

One entertainment during the conference was a barbecue, such as I have never seen nor hope to see again for it turned me into a vegetarian. The central alfresco set consisted in three huge bonfires stacked as pyramids against which were complete cattle corpses, each severed and spread like a spatchcock with legs protruding. The stench of burning, roasting flesh was ghastly. Gauchos on horseback galloped and reared through the assembled company, shouting and wielding long knives, a performance of virile male exhibitionism.

As they approached the fires they slashed a piece of roasting flesh and presented it to you on the end of their knives while others brought goblets of deep red wine, cabernet sauvignon only darker. The sight of the striated meat, muscle and fat, let alone mouthful of it, was revolting. I was overcome with disgust and John was almost as affected. We had to stick it out for we were guests in the middle of a ranch somewhere and could only get back to semi-civilisation in the coaches provided.

It was with relief that we left Buenos Aires and made for Bolivia. You will know as we did, intellectually, that Bolivia is 4000 metres high, Andes country. The knowledge turned actual on disembarking from the plane at La Paz airport for the knees of the woman in front of me buckled with oxygen deprivation as she descended in a heap to the tarmac. The thin air hit us all. Despite chewing the coca leaves provided, local defence against altitude nausea, one by one our entire party took to their beds, myself one of the last.

And did we feel ill! The worst kind of hangover. John and I managed one event before succumbing, for it was Thanksgiving Day, a day regarded by Dorothy as sacrosanct, her mid-Atlantic stance leaning USA-ward each fourth Thursday in November. Ever since she became part of our lives turkey, cranberry sauce and pumpkin pie had to be the menu with a stars and stripes somewhere on the table. So, a telephone call from a public phone booth on what seemed like a deserted track in a quiet spot above La Paz to wish her Happy Thanksgiving, preceded John and I walking slowly and breathlessly to our hotel and silent suffering Europeans. As I lay in an altitude sickness haze I was just aware of the intense blue/black night sky with not a sound, utter silence, just from time to time dogs calling to each other.

So began what was a sensational trip, starting alongside Lake Titicaca, with its ornate reed boats and reed-tented settlements, hugging the lake. Leaning back in the coach, breathing deeply, chewing coca leaves, I glanced at the local women in their bowler hats, billowing skirts and embroidered shawls tending their llama herds and guinea pig farms. The men's chests had become barrel shaped, as over generations their lungs adapted to the altitude. We did not adapt very well at all. As far as I could see everyone's hangover continued. So to Puno, still horizontal, our hotel built apparently of condensed sand, utterly silent.

Relief came at last with the gentle zig-zig descent by rickety local train, blessedly easing our nausea, taking us to our destination, miraculous world-famous ruins of the Inca city, Machu Picchu. Perhaps because back home we were focused on the steep cut terraces at Beechmont I had a fellow feeling with the Incas who had chiselled and built stone walls to save their city from falling down the mountain side. But they had only hand-held tools while we could hire a crane and a dumper and a stone wall builder.

On to Cusco where the layers of history embedded in its fabric told the tale of the Spanish conquistador's rape of the Inca culture, and modern Peruvians 'improvements' of Pizarro's palatial architecture. Hooray for history. It sets one's little problems in a broader context.

Two years later, but now travelling on my own without John, I was invited to the University of Iowa and I should have declined. Four years later, this time to Brock University in Canada, the same applies. The problem was that both were Physical Education departments working from my first book of 1963, and I had of course moved on radically in the twenty years. They expected me to speak on that material. Worse, in Brock they had embraced an interpretation of Laban's ideas using them for creative gymnastics, reducing the expressivity of his work to quasi-inventive functionality. My dilemma was, should I give them an affirmation of what they were doing, or speak my mind, the latter of course is what I did. Ah well.

What I discovered in Iowa as a by-product was the world's largest collection on Dada, the avant-garde nihilistic performance art movement of the WW1 years in Zurich. In Iowa? Was that possible? It was; manuscripts, objects, photographs. Since Laban's dancers participated in the Dada furore I was intrigued. Although not yet contemplating writing his biography this collection was gold dust. Before long the collector, Stephen Foster, was planning a book. He invited me to contribute a chapter which I did, 'Bodies in Dada', for which my fairly new perspective of the sociology and politics of the flesh were invaluable.

Much more comfortable than Brock was an invitation to Reggio Emilia to a Forsythe festival. I knew little about William Forsythe but he knew and was blown apart by Laban's ideas. Forsythe, earlier with the Joffrey and Stuttgart Ballets, now startling choreographer at Frankfurt, had in the last couple of years found a way of making astonishing new movement by seeing ballet as 'living architecture' rather than a fixed vocabulary of steps. He had found the concept in Laban's text *Choreutics* and being the insightful artist he was, he ran with the idea where others before him had not seen its potential. Forsythe insisted that the city festival in his honour should include a Laban day conference.

My good fortune was that the chairperson, Professor Eugenia Casini Ropa from Bologna had invited me to give workshops at her University a few years before. I was invited to speak on Laban in an open discussion with Forsythe. I learned as much as he did for I was left with another entrée into Laban's culture looking at it with an artist's eye, the eye of a choreographer in search of new methods, which is of course exactly what Laban himself was.

Some years later, with a research grant, I looked at one of Forsythe's works in detail, *The Loss of Small Detail*, an hour-long multi-media work of astounding invention. But at this point I returned home to find John very unwell.

The line up for the Reggio Emilia Rudolf Laban Conference. Third from left scholars Eugenia Casini Ropa & Donatella Bertozi, VP-D, film maker Eva Elisabeth Fischer (Ph. Nigel Voak)

John and me looking down at Cusco from the monumental ruins of Sacsayhuaman

Machu Picchu terraces with John on the eighth terrace

CHAPTER 16

1984

John's Demise

It is hardly possible but I still receive a stocking from Father Christmas filled with all manner of delicious and personal packages, including champagne, the reindeer bringing it is my impossibly generous daughter, Emma. As a Quaker we don't treat Christmas Day as any different from any other day which I cannot believe is a good idea since it is impossible not to see that it is different. In any event I make it different by going to Midnight Mass at Southwark Cathedral, my father's cathedral, and visit his memorial chair in the retro chapel.

I dropped into the cathedral recently, walking along the Thames Path from The Royal Festival Hall, and there on this ecclesiastic chair curled up and asleep was the cathedral mog. The citation above reads In Memory of Arthur Llewellyn Preston 'A man much beloved'. It pleased me that this corner which could be dark and neglected was far from it with the chair heated by hot pipes and clearly the luxury home to a stray cat. Bill would have liked that being a man who loved the ordinary things of life.

The memorial chair organised by my father's brothers replaced a more sinister one, The Consistory Chair upon which in the past a Bishop would sit in pomp judging recalcitrant churchmen brought before him for their misdemeanours. In Tudor times punishments were dire including burning at the stake so hooray that that old chair has gone, together with its whiff of purgatory.

Christmases at Beechmont were stupendous and shared with all manner of people. At the bottom of the drive John had planted a fir tree that became our Christmas Tree. With the gardener's help we all decorated it with fairy lights. On Christmas Eve all and sundry came to the house for carols and mince pies. It was a large gathering ranging from the suffragan Bishop of Tonbridge and his wife to the helpers at the Clubs, swimmers, dancers, musicians, Uncle Tom Cobley and All.

Our spacious entrance hall was filled with wine-drinking guests for the carols with the overflow sitting on the circular staircase overlooking the crib. Made by Roger from Smarty packs, 'sticky backed plastic', bottle tops, pipe cleaners, under the tutelage of TVs *Blue Peter*, the crib is set up annually in my sitting room to this day. With Emma on recorder to give us the starting note we sang lustily and harmoniously as many guests were in the G and S operas and were playing members of the music club. We caroled and imbibed and celebrated until it was time for midnight mass, after tucking up the children on pain of death to sleep before Father Christmas came.

The usual joyous family things went on over Christmas morning, led by Roger who bicycled down to the church, picking up wayward cousin Mary Mary on the way. Between them they 'bagged' the front pew for Elizabeth's and our family to occupy. I was never quite sure about the democracy of that but the children were so pleased that I let it go. We sang again and wished everyone in the bursting congregation Happy Christmas and returned to stuff the bird, put sixpences in the Christmas pudding, eat, and collect in the sitting room to open our presents.

It was at this moment in 1983 that something catastrophic happened. Roger and Emma and I each had our presents on a chair but John held his on his lap. The young and I undid our parcels with whoops of joy but John remained still. The whole event took its usual time and the young seemed unperturbed. I said nothing, wondering what was going through John's head. 'Time for TV', I suggested and away they went to the playroom. John remained, his presents still unwrapped. I waited for him to speak.

Eventually he said, 'It's no use,' and went upstairs.

What did he mean? What was wrong? I felt a mixture of bewilderment and anger. Why behave like that on Christmas Day? John was never good at talking about anything with emotional content. He lay on his bed saying nothing, leaving me floundering. Poor man, all he knew was that somehow his head would not function. So began two years in which he changed from being a highly successful professional man into one overwhelmed by an incomprehensible mental state of uncertainty with the anxiety that he might make a mistake for a client with disastrous consequences.

Mental illness is understood far better now than it was thirty years ago. With less obvious symptoms than in my own breakdown, the doctors were guessing. One thought he might be depressed (about what?) and said three months off work. His partners thought he was skiving (why would he?). If it was depression I knew what that felt like and it was only too physically real. But John had no loss of voice, no visor that came down, no horror of noise and colour, so I was at a loss. Should I leave him to rest, or cajole him into action? Should I suggest a holiday? Or find a therapist?

John went back to work, monitored by a partner, but it was no good. He could not distinguish what was detail from what was essential in an invention. So he had to resign from his firm and from his Presidency of the Chartered Institute feeling as he did that he had completely let down his colleagues and his family.

I had to act immediately for in one black hole we lost his substantial income. Clearly we could not afford to continue all the Beechmont activities John had supported. What about the Studio? The clubs? The pool? The music? The garden? We would lose the two gardeners, the housekeeper, the au pair, the studio manager and I would have to increase to full-time employment at the Laban Centre just to pay the daily bills. Within six months, in shock, beloved Beechmont, the cottage, the studio, were for sale.

Maybe it was because as a six year old I had been through tumultuous change I was able to weather the storm and say: that's how it is, get on with it. But the family? John had already fully done for Roger, at eighteen, what a father could, got him a good education and discussed ideas on what he might proceed to as a career. For Emma, at thirteen, a vulnerable age, it was much more difficult. I imagined her coming home from school to a mentally unwell father, me at work, and came to the conclusion that that was such an unpredictable scenario that she might be better in a boarding school. Emma, just as I had at thirteen, found herself away from home, at this crucial point and, just as I had, she found it awful.

With Beechmont in the midst of being sold, while we lived temporarily in the cottage, Roger and I took off for Australia, as another chapter recounts. The paradox was that while John's career shattered mine was taking off. In a way how good that it was, it meant finance for the family was less a worrying issue but it exaggerated for John his decline and loneliness as off I went, to Sydney when he needed me to be there, for him, in his crisis. And I wasn't.

We looked for a house as different as possible from Beechmont, possibly nearer the Laban Centre, since I would have to spend my days there. In the end I bought a flat in Blackheath as a pied-à-terre for late evening work and found a family house in Ightham village, a black and white Tudor house built in 1480. We named it Corners for it was in fact a house with two cottages attached giving it an L-shape with three twisting staircases and an inglenook fireplace. One staircase led to a self-contained flat, ideal for Roger as he found his feet as an adult. By a strategically-placed gong at the bottom of his stairs we could request entry and he could deny it if he were entertaining his friends and doing what young people do. We were all for the inevitable experiments and mistakes to be made in the safety of home. Four years later it was Emma's turn to try out her lifestyle, her friends, her mistakes, as Roger set his foot on the very bottom of the property ladder.

John's demise was to stay with him, gradually and irreversibly taking hold. My idea was to find a cure for him, I held to the futile belief that he must be curable. That seemed possible for his condition wasn't stable and he was sometimes better. Then down with a crash and a period of total inactivity or worse in hospital. Hospital staff, kind as they were, tried electric shock treatment. In all he had twenty. Did they do any good? No. The local GP put us on to Behavioural Therapy for a Personality Disorder. While John stayed upstairs all day long I took him up a cup of tea, a sandwich. 'Leave him without food. He will come down when he is hungry,' instructed the therapist as if John were a naughty school boy who needed to be taught a lesson. One time when Dorothy was staying with us, she asked him where he felt ill. 'It's not there, it's here,' he said, holding his head.

It wasn't Alzheimers for he never lost touch with his memory but it was a slow collapse of the bit of the brain that deals with imagination. You don't realise it but you imagine what you are going to do before you do it and if the brain won't imagine it you can't do it. Years later, lying on his bed, in Drake Court Care Home it went like this:

'John, shall we go for a walk?' He raised his eyebrows.

'Shall we get ready?' He raised his eyebrows.

'How about sitting up?' I gave him my hands and he sat up.

'What about a coat?' He raised his eyebrows.
I showed him the sleeve and he put his arm into it.

I gave him my hands and he stood up and together we went downstairs and out. Out was a fearful place for John because it offered decisions that he couldn't take. Should we turn right or left, shall we cross the road? So, essentially, holding each other, we had to take exactly the same route every walk since somehow he remembered the way and that was the way he must take. I think he enjoyed it. He never said so but he agreed to do it again next week.

John's decline was slow, it took ten years before he needed residential care. We had many happy times in the meantime, occasionally as if he were well and my heart leapt, perhaps, perhaps he was recovering? I just had to discover that he could do less and less of his own volition but if I laid something straightforward out for him he could function. What was so ghastly to witness was his attempts to lead a normal life that failed. He was cast in *The Beggar's Opera*, his tenor voice being just right, but he couldn't master the moves or remember the routines, so he resigned. He joined a Scottish reel club but again couldn't master the steps and left.

In the meantime I went to work, to the Laban Centre, to teach, research, rehearse, tutor. I had to leave him on his own with instructions for the day. Sometimes he managed well, at others I would find him lying on the sofa having achieved almost nothing and he would say, 'I ran out of puff,' as I set to on the breakfast washing-up.

I describe amassing the Laban Collection in another chapter, entailing as it did travelling all over Europe gathering historical material. I managed to get a sort of job for John at the Laban Centre cataloguing in its archive as I brought in the booty from the trips to Europe, programmes, advertisements, letters, books, photos, legal documents, all manner of memorabilia of Laban's life and work in Europe. To safeguard them in those days they were photographed for sheets of negatives, then processed for students and scholars to study on a viewing machine. It required meticulous detailed work that I could induct John into and he would do it as I flew from one studio to another teaching and rehearsing.

Eventually I was advised that residential care would be kinder for him so he went to a private house nearby with three 'residents'. I went to see him as often as possible juggling my timetable as best I could. By this time

I had the flat in Blackheath ten minutes from the Laban Centre, so I could work all morning with an early start, rush down to John for a walk, then back to the Laban Centre for late lectures and sleep at Blackheath.

Before long a crisis for him developed and he was taken into Maidstone Hospital. I found him there in the Psychiatric Assessment Unit on suicide watch. I was mortified to discover that over the two years he had lost more than two stone and I hadn't realised it, a gradual diminishing, as apparently he ate less and less.

John was sectioned which meant he must live in locked accommodation. I continued to visit him everyday, even for a few minutes, just to keep him going. One afternoon some weeks later the specialist said, 'We can't do any more for him. You must let him go,' he said. What! 'You can't lead his life for him.' He would be discharged in two weeks and I must find him a secure care home by then. Having more capital than allowed to qualify for state care I was given no guidance. Where do I find an EMI home? Elderly Mental Infirm. That's up to you, they said. Having private means we were not their responsibility. One felt like a pariah.

So began two weeks of awfulness as I scoured the district visiting locked homes. They were ghastly, the stench of urine overwhelming, the incapacity and confusion of the inmates hard to witness. 'I can't send John to one of these,' called my crying heart. Thankfully they were all full. Widening my search I eventually located a vacancy at a newly-opened smallish home run by a young couple but in Herne Bay. Where is that?

Forty-five miles from Ightham, sixty from Blackheath. Oh God, I thought, how will I visit him, how will I keep touch with him? And in my audacity, how will he manage if I am not nearby?

He did manage as his arena gradually diminished, closing in, his life centred on his bed, his place, his safe haven. Down I drove every Sunday; walked we did on the sea front, whatever the weather, past the slot machines and fish and chips, the boarding houses and cheap cafés. Five years he was there, two hundred and sixty once-a-week trips, two hundred and sixty identical walks. There came a time when the speeding fines I accrued topped the limit. The A2 was becoming the M2, the 50 mph patches changing each week. Tired and miserable at the end of the visit my concentration waned. I was caught on camera too many times.

To get him up to Blackheath became essential but the homes there were not EMI registered. So began a battle to get him de-sectioned. The National Health was not used to such a request. My darling man was a danger to no one, or to himself. I eventually succeeded and up he came to Drake Court, a converted stately home on the Blackheath Park estate. Suffice it to say he lived there reasonably contented, eventually lying on his bed all day, with the door open so he could see people passing.

Our once-a-week walks continued, in Greenwich Park. I was there today, with my Disabled Parking blue badge and walking stick, taking my constitutional, feeding the squirrels, counting the deer, surrounded by ghosts of Nanny pushing me in my pram, she in uniform, I in my velvet-collared coat, and John and I, hand in hand.

John at Roger and Venetia's wedding five years into his illness

John and me walking in
Greenwich Park in the last
year of his life

The grandchildren sitting
on Bill's Consistory Chair in
Southwark Cathedral with
Roger and Venetia

CHAPTER 17

1985

Scholarly Endeavours

I have given up long-haul flights, they are not compatible with the octogenarian body. I enjoy lying back in the garden lazily scanning the vapour trails from Heathrow as the workers of the world make their transcontinental commute. One of them might be Roger for I never know which country he is in. With widespread commitments he is permanently airborne with a carbon footprint I shudder to contemplate. I consider my flying history when as Dr Preston-Dunlop rather than Mrs John Dunlop I started to travel abroad on my own business, with New York one of the early destinations.

Before a doctorate you have to have achieved a good MA and for me, with no formal education under my belt since leaving school at sixteen I was required to take an Advanced Diploma to be accepted on a Master's course. I would be on familiar ground, I thought, for it focused on educational principles. It took me back to the damp-cloth-on-forehead months with Margaret Rosewarne when I struggled with how to embed theories of learning that she was studying into Rudolf Laban's inspiring but not-useful-enough book *Modern Educational Dance*.

Having got to grips with Piaget then, it was Emil Durkheim I had to digest now and the sociological ideas he promoted, new and exciting to me. I had hardly heard of sociology but was confronted with notions of 'sociology of the body', 'politics of the body', 'the subversive nature of the body' and started to look afresh at my own flesh and blood and what I did with them/it. No wonder conceptual learning is valued over practical learning of the body, I learnt, when you think of the words we choose as expletives 'shit and fuck, cunt and dick'. My polite family life, my ecclesiastic background, John's Presbyterian schooldays, were worlds away from this, but eye-opening. My brain reeled with philosophy of education, psychology of learning, epistemology, translating what these things might mean for dance and for designing a BA (Hons) in Dance Theatre, and getting out of Physical Education.

The current buzz in the arts colleges, here and in the USA, was 'Are the arts languages?' Many an intriguing tome was written by philosophers teasing that question out. As a keen new academic, soon with an MA, keeping abreast, as it were, of current thinking I had written an experimental text entitled *Dance is a Language isn't it?* Its form broke just about every rule, written as if each page were a dance space with words appearing all over the place, so to speak choreographing the page. Pages were typed on a family caravan holiday, with Roger and Emma helping. Marion North decided that *Dance: A Linguistic Approach* might be a more suitable title in an institution reaching for academic recognition but somehow the title page she added, without consultation, always went missing...?

Teaching in the Laban Centre could be hazardous as Marion miraculously expanded the temporary premises, simply a hopelessly inadequate adapted primary school, by obtaining the adjacent and vacant St James Church. Its transformation into spaces of all shapes, sizes and functions was not finished on schedule. The new academic year started with ladders in place of a staircase. Donning metaphorical steel hats we carried on such was the spirit that here, at the Laban Centre, something worthwhile was taking place. With the old churchyard transparently roofed it became an atrium joining school to church, a place to meet, discuss, plan things new, a wonderfully creative space. In Studio 6, a space that retained some of its ecclesiastic architecture, including a wooden bishop's seat embedded in a stone wall, I could not help but imagine my father in this place. Did he take a confirmation service here, or baptise babies, marry couples, as part of his responsibilities as Bishop of Woolwich?

Marion and I had an unusual collegiate relationship, we needed each other. We shared the aim to establish dance practice as capable of being seen as scholarly to replace the view held by academia generally that dance was a twinkle-toes activity, certainly not worthy of degree status, no, master's degree, dear me no, doctorate, laughable and impossible, but, I was on the way to getting one, the first in the UK. I recall when I applied to be allowed to study for a Master's Degree, I was vetted by a mathematics professor at London University. He could not understand how a woman who left school at sixteen, a dancer to boot, could be so audacious as to wish to enter his domain of academia. He literally advised that I should go home and look after my children. It gave me great pleasure five years later to invite him to the award ceremony of my doctorate, but he didn't come. Coward.

One man who was intrigued by the topic of my book was New Yorker Robert Ellis Dunn, the spirit behind the extraordinary and experimental Judson Church Theater Collective. Yvonne Rainer, Deborah Hay, Steve Paxton, Trisha Brown, were questioning every value thought to be sacred to choreographic works, meaning, technique, dynamic phrasing, entertainment... Could linguistics throw light on this New York phenomenon, the Judson hiatus? At least a spoken language has a receiver, a listener, an audience, a respondent, and it seemed to some as if the Judson Collective were ignoring theirs. Somehow I was invited to lead a linguistics course set up by the Dance Notation Bureau so off I went to New York and Robert Dunn attended.

I don't believe I did a very good job, it is never easy to land in a new culture and get it just right, the language barrier between Americans and the English exists. But my mix of dance practice, academic study and dance writing stood me in good enough stead to be invited again the following year. Sadly the Mayflower Hotel adjacent to Central Park and the Lincoln Centre is no more. It offered me my first Manhattan in the bar and a 'sunny side up' breakfast egg.

My first book *A Handbook for Modern Educational Dance* had become *the* text in Australia although it was by now twenty years old. So hot on New York I accepted the invitation to speak at a Physical Education gathering if I could bring Roger along with me for he was in his gap year after finishing school. What better way to widen his horizons than visit the other side of the world. Off we went together, first to Singapore where we did the tourist trail, a rickshaw in the rain across town for a Singapore Sling in the colonial Raffles Hotel, a *tian tian* chicken rice and *char kway teow*, with chopsticks in China Town and a heavenly visit to the tropical orchid farm.

In Sydney we stayed in a private house in the suburbs, home to a welcoming couple, with two sons of Roger's age whose one idea was to taunt him as a spineless Pommie.

They met their match for one thing Roger was not was a coward. Up coast lay a well-known testing ground for the young male, a bay with a forty-foot drop into the sea. This spineless Pommie was invited to jump. 'I will if you will,' he said. 'You first,' they said, and he jumped and they did not follow. It was a long way down, down, down and the IMPACT on the water was a shock. The only way back was scarier still through an underwater tunnel. Thank goodness for a watchful coastguard posted there to save the lives of teenagers. 'Grab on to my foot, breathe in and hold your breath, *Now*,' he said. Before Roger could think they swam underwater through the only route out of the bay. The boys had never had the guts to jump so the tide turned for Pommie Roger's stay.

I also had a bit of a shock for the new craze hitting Australian Physical Education was aerobics and they hoped I would include aerobics in my speech. I certainly could not. The creative dance I represented, a sensitive, expressive, collaborative, art form was in direct opposition to this new treatment of the body as a health-needy object. The experience accelerated my energies to get dance out of Physical Education where it still was (and sometimes is) in the British education system. When will men ever learn that the body has other ways of expressing itself than competitive sport?

My hosts invited me to The Club, the social centre of their housing development, with every kind of sport and restaurant available, plus, in the centre, a casino. Behind each betting machine stood a silent line of people waiting their turn to gamble. I could not believe that this was the pride and joy of the district, the chosen activity for the weekend but it was. We returned home, Roger still with a bruised backside from hitting the sea at speed and I with determination to get on with my education and arm myself with the teeth needed to nip the heels of Physical Education.

Home at this point, temporarily, was Beechmont Cottage, while the main house was being sold. I had thought how awful to live in our own gardener's accommodation but we loved it. The garage became my study and I needed one to finish *Point of Departure*, a technical book full of drawings, signs and symbols on how geometric lines can be used in dance as a template to find new sequences of movement. I had commissioned an artist, Margot Longden, to illustrate creative ways of using the book and that led to another example of a crunch between family and work.

It started like this, 'Mum, do you think we could have a hot Sunday lunch?' A polite way of saying Mum, it really is about time you did some family cooking. 'Yes of course,' I said and took a chicken out of the freezer. What I had forgotten was that I had booked the artist for midday. As I contemplated the naked bird, Margot with sketch pad in hand, arrived. Dilemma, do I send her away and cook Sunday lunch as any reasonable mother/wife might or find another solution? I needed the illustrations for the book in time for imminent publication, so: 'Emma, here is a chicken, and here is a cook book and I'll be back in an hour.' I hotfooted to the Studio with Margot while Emma learned to make coq au vin. She is now, I may say, a vegetarian.

Last week sitting in the stalls of the Lyttleton Theatre on the South Bank my neighbour turned out to be half way through a cerebral doctorate on the Brontës, earnestly devouring the before-show talk by director Sally Cookson on *Jane Eyre,* a superbly imaginative transfer of book to stage. It took me back to my earnest days, on returning to the Laban Centre from trips abroad, when my own doctorate research was in mid-stream. Unlike my Lyttleton neighbour I was determined to show that a research activity could be more than purely cerebral, could reveal a gap in both knowledge and choreographic methods addressed rigorously through dance practice itself. Thank heaven for my tutor, Dorothy, whose PhD was the first in dance with practice. While some of the academics at the Laban Centre shuddered at the idea of practice as research, making their views known vociferously, we paid no attention and proved them wrong. Of course I undertook formal analysis of other choreographers' works and made use of a new computer tool to overlay curves and lines onto a film of a dance to highlight the patterns the movement contained, laborious, innovative, and revealing.

Going for a Walk with a Line was the title of the doctoral dance suite I choreographed with faculty members as the dancers and a commissioned score for clarinet and keyboard. Paul Klee had created with lines and forms in his experimental abstract paintings. I was able to project his modernist images as the backdrop. Of the five sections, one duo worked as a piece of theatre, *Rounding,* not only because of my earnestly researched movement material but partly by the casting, a Japanese man, strong and dark, with a petite Portuguese woman.

She engaged in all manner of isolated curving moves, in shoulder, head, heel, elbow, in unexpected rhythms, centre stage, with no connection to the man. He, at a distance, mirrored their roundness in larger slower moves derived from her material, some parallel to hers, some inverted. As he gradually circled around her he created a theatrical tension, an anticipation of whether he would approach her or not. Thank you beautiful dancers and Paul Klee for your haunting image.

With a doctorate in dance under my belt, the first in the United Kingdom with practice, all manner of opportunities opened up, not only for me but for the Laban Centre. For all Marion's awkwardness and bloody-mindedness she was a magnificent leader, steering her ship in new directions that kept the Laban Centre ahead of the game, with the first BA in Dance in the UK, the first MA in Dance, the first doctorate programme.

My invitations abroad were confined to Europe for the next five years and were tricky. Thanks to Dorothy's close connections in France, she with impeccable French, I was asked to give a course on 'Laban et son Heritage' despite my unimpeccable French. The French people have a love/hate relationship with anything German but also a respect for rationality, so it was his theories of 3D spatial forms in dance that won the day as the dancers embodied harmonic patterns in beautifully executed movement that somehow had something profound to say.

Next up Berlin, for a centenary conference on Mary Wigman. The tension between devotees of Laban and devotees of Wigman is legendary, initiated by Wigman herself. She vowed while studying with him in Monte Verita that since she was not attractive to him sexually, as was every other woman he met, she would beat him as a choreographer and dance innovator. A woman spurned is a dangerous animal and Laban's cartoons of her are truly unkind. She did indeed become a colossal figure in German dance in the 1920s and 1930s but so did he, so I knew that I should tread carefully in Berlin. Luckily my German language stood me in good stead and I passed muster.

On to Essen for a theatre scholars' conference and Arles for an international dance conference. Here I was on stronger ground, I thought, as the concepts and methods of my doctorate were scholarly and new. I introduced the term 'choreology', on a par with musicology. Although it is a word with obvious meaning, the 'ology' of dance, it had not been in use. I came to use it through an interview with choreographic giant Aurel Milloss in Rome. Telling him what we were trying to do for dance in the minefield of academia in the UK he stood up, being a dramatic man, gesticulated and said '*Ciò che stai insegnando è coreologia*', ie, you are teaching choreology. It was a term first used for dance theory in Laban's 1930s research centre in Berlin where Milloss had become a student, a time that changed his life.

My struggle in the UK was that philosophers, sociologists, aestheticians, historians, were looking *at* dance from the outside, bringing their own methodologies. These needed to be balanced, in my view, by equally strong studies of dance from within, using our own methodologies, for the study of the material of dance itself, its rhythms and forms, its vocabularies, choreographic methods and performance. I was on the way to establishing Choreological Studies as that, but the Essen academics were defensive seeing something they knew nothing about promoted as an ology, on a par with their domains. I tried it out again in Arles in a room full of dance critics and historians and the result was a very muted interest. Ah well. But ten years later Choreological Studies was a core subject at Trinity Laban and its postgraduates now take choreology all over the world so persistence is rewarded. My *Dance and the Performative: a choreological perspective* (2004) is read widely. I have seen it on the reading list of an American University dance department and in Hong Kong. So thank you Milloss.

My next more comfortable arenas were conferences with workshops: Bayreuth on 'German Expressionist Dance' with Laban the leader and Wigman the rival, Brussels on 'Deep Learning', dance as a form of practical research, Bologna on 'Laban the Man and his Work', Rotterdam, Helsinki and Antwerp on 'Choreological Methods for Choreographers.' All these institutions were sympathetic to dance as both an art and a mode of research, such a relief from battling in institutions where the twinkle toes image gets in the way.

In between these forays, back to the home front, supporting Roger in his pursuit of love, watching him being headhunted as he climbed the work ladder, helping Emma into the university of her choice and listening delighted as her soprano voice showed its full colours, and supporting John as best I could for by now his tragic illness had taken hold.

The original (red) cover of *Dance is a Language isn't it?*

Image capture from the research film of 'Rounding' from *Going for a Walk with a Line*

Research film hand drawing the curves the dancer makes around her body, a pioneering method in 1981 but now easily drawn electronically

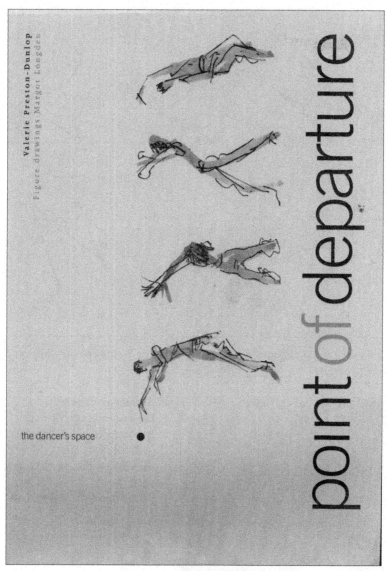

Cover (yellow) of *Point of Departure* with Margot Longden's illustrations

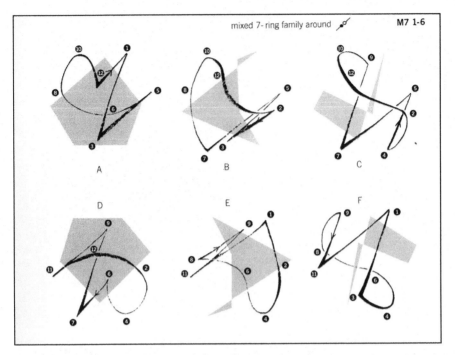

mixed 7-ring family around   M7 1-6

Diagrams of the zig-zag and surrounding curve of 7-rings as they appear in *Point of Departure*

About to rehearse a presentation on Nijinska's *Les Noces* (see the Bride's long plaits on the floor) in one of the new studios in St James' with faculty members Jean Jarrell and Dale Thompson

Aurel Milloss in 1928 with fellow students and faculty at the Berlin
Choreographisches Institut after Laban presented his new notation method to
the dance profession (Laban Collection)

CHAPTER 18

1986

Europe, Here I Come

This weekend sisterly duties called, to aid Elizabeth for a day event at East Grinstead Hospital famed for its pioneering work with plastic surgery. As a teenager in the latter years of WW2 I had done my bit of war work here, in the kitchens, as the surgeons attempted to create new faces, new hands on horribly burnt airmen. Their appalling disfigurements were a gruesome sight for a young person but they were encouraged to face the world and the local town to embrace their courage. 'McIndoe's Guinea Pigs' they were called, as he experimented with reconstructive surgery. I waited for Elizabeth in The Hurricane Café while down the corridor The Spitfire Restaurant reminded us of the wartime heritage.

Driving back in the dark we skirted Gatwick Airport, a place of many memories for me. One set of journeys came about by an invitation to give workshops in Paris out of which came a joyous few years as a jury member for Choreography Competitions. The Fédération Francaise de Danse, led in Paris by Mireille Delsout, ran gatherings for up and coming choreographers to show their work, win a prize, or not, and receive a critique of their oeuvres. Dorothy was also a jury member being a doyenne of French dance taste with her skill of mentoring in Maryland University and her affinity with French culture. Before long the competitions became the Fédération Internationale de Danse (FID). I had the good fortune of becoming the British representative on the jury. It seemed that the sweat and toil of doctorate research into choreographic methods stood me in good stead as I attempted to share what I saw and suggest how the work might say and do what it was intended to say and do.

What better way to spend a weekend than with like-minded people watching innovative dance in La Rochelle, Toulouse, Istres, Bruges, dining in delightful restaurants, breathing in the continental air and testing ones ability to mentor young artists. From time to time I listen, along with a *pichet de vin,* to French cabaret songs recorded by Marie Jo, the eventual Directrice de la Fédération Internationale de Danse, her voice a throaty mix of Jean Sablon and Edith Piaf. Vive la France!

An observer on these competitive events was a Dutchman, director of the state sponsored amateur dance organisation of the Netherlands. In the main Holland took the view, and maybe still does, that choreography is a given talent that cannot be taught but his organisation took another view, to my advantage. So began regular visits for week-long workshops in Holland for aspiring dance artists where I was tested to show that the craftsmanship of choreography, and the techniques of critiquing and mentoring a work, can indeed be transmitted.

An invitation came to judge the more prestigious competition at Bagnolet, Paris where choreographers further in their careers than at the FID showed their dances. Some gained work opportunities from the outcome so jurying carried much responsibility.

Choreographers who had come through the first auditions could claim shortlisting and those that won could expect commissions. Darting over to Paris daily via the much-loved London City Airport, to see the show, darting back to the Laban Centre for student examinations made a complex week but, heyho, it made for an interesting life.

In between these endeavours I returned to the home front, to Ightham. Roger was establishing himself in the housing market, articulate, focused, doing well, while John tried to keep himself going helping his aged and failing aunt Glen, and the luckless Emma languished in boarding school. I flew in and out and hotfooted it to London, to the Laban Centre, the latter known to all who worked there as the salt mines.

Marion North, between 1972, when she took over the reins, and the mid 1980s, was achieving the impossible by transforming a failing school into an international leader in the field, a feat that left casualties en route. Luckily for me I was not one of them primarily because I served her purpose. When not in France or Holland, I was collecting archival materials on Laban in Germany, or Switzerland, or Austria, whichever was the next promising hunting ground. What I found was a stark indication that in his time 1920–1936 he had been a giant, the philosophical and creative powerhouse of *Der neue Tanz* or *Ausdruckstanz*. As is known the Nazi regime had deliberately and successfully annihilated his name when they realised he would not serve their purpose.

The Laban Collection is the name for this mass of material I found in Europe which I would not have looked for if Lisa Ullmann and I had been on better terms. My strained relations with Lisa came to a head as she lay dying as far from bequeathing Rudolf Laban's British estate to the Laban Centre, as in his will, she left it all to the University of Surrey. Convinced that the critique of the man's work that I was undertaking was unnecessary she determined that his legacy should remain ossified, exactly as he had left it. While Marion North battled to save the Laban Centre from financial difficulties by espousing possible mergers with academia, Goldsmiths College for one, it was essential that an institution with the name Laban should have an archive holding of his work.

I rushed to Lisa's hospital bedside, not knowing if she would see me or not. 'I am going to collect evidence of his pre-war work in Europe,' I said, 'where shall I start?' Hardly able to speak she whispered, 'Go to Vienna. Find Klingenbeck.' Who is that, I asked myself, but John and I did go to Vienna and we found Klingenbeck.

Now an elderly *Intendant* of one of the smaller Viennese theatres, Fritz Klingenbeck had worked with Laban for ten years as dancer and notation aid. Although confused he had a personal archive with photographs. During three days, nudging his memory, he was able to set me on an adventure that took me to Switzerland, Austria, Paris, Belgium, Germany, Italy, Croatia, Norway, finding evidence in city after city where Tanzbühne Laban had performed, where Laban had danced, lectured, lived, struggled, succeeded and finally fled.

Having recently returned to Gatwick Airport after a sybaritic week on the Cote D'Azur my mind turned to the planes I had taken from there to collect the Laban archive, regularly over three years. If the place of search were French-speaking Dorothy accompanied me to aid my schoolgirl French. If it were German-speaking John came for he was better at old German script than was I and despite his illness could be a real help.

On one occasion Dorothy and I flew to Zurich and found the village where Laban lived in a *ménage à trois* during WW1 and where, with his wife Maja on one arm and his lover Susi Perrottet on the other, he witnessed the noisy anarchic tumultuous Dada performances at the Cabaret Voltaire. Susi had just died and her daughter-in-law's house was filled with Susi's French jottings including letters to and from Laban that revealed gold dust, the day-to-day developments of 1912 when he first began his researches into dance. We hot-footed down to the photocopy machine with pages and pages in Laban's hand including his wicked cartoons of his voluptuous affair with Susi, his lampooning of the unseductive Mary Wigman, with Maja depicted as a jealous cat. Ah well, men will be men.

One visit, with John and Emma, took us to Basle to find ninety-year-old Käthe Wulff, an outspoken dancer with Laban in the Dada years. She gave me a private lesson, she seated in black beating her drum and gong as I responded to her instructions, swooping, swirling, speeding, shaping, creeping, still. Somehow we found we had booked ourselves into a brothel, with mirrors above the bed and a dark corridor to a section of the hotel lit in deep crimson with scantily-clad ladies. A bar within revealed recumbent figures overwhelmed by the local ale. We slept all three in the bed for Emma's safety and fled the next morning. I could not help glancing towards the 5-star hotel where John and I had stayed as guests on his professional visits to Swiss Aluminium, another world, another time.

We shot out of the brothel to meet up with Beatrice Loeb in her fairly lavish home. An erstwhile student of Laban's Choreographisches Institut in Berlin she had become a wealthy donor of Laban's work in the UK. Clearly in his younger days Laban had captured the heart of many a woman. One such was Herta Feist whom I tracked down in a nunnery aged ninety-two. She had led a brilliant Laban dance school in Berlin in the 1930s but was overcome with remorse at her own collaboration with the Nazi cause and had decided to withdraw to silence. She never said a word in answer to my questions. It was after that visit that archivist and historian Kurt Peters advised me: 'Don't ask for we won't tell.' The memories and the guilt were just too painful. How lucky we were in Britain that we did not have the Nazi question unavoidably close.

A poster of the *Chat Noir* cabaret of 1900 that faces me on my study wall as I type reminds me of a trip I took with Dorothy accompanied by her admirer, Roland, an *acteur*, to St Maurice, a Parisian suburb by the Bois de Vincennes. There we searched for and found the modest home where Laban had lodged his first wife, he himself living mainly in his artist's *atelier* in the Boulevard Montparnasse for he was a bohemian, a student at the prestigious Écoles des Beaux Arts.

We found the birth certificates of their two children and with excitement asked for a photocopy of each, an innocent request. No such thing. The French are sensitive about birthright and inheritance presuming that we were seeking to claim legitimacy.

Roland came to our aid. In his impeccable French he declaimed, dramatically, that Dorothy was a well-connected American researcher who must be obliged. With the original documents in our hands we sped to the Mairie, to the *chef legale*. At *cinq minutes* to the sacred hour of *le déjeuner*, he succumbed to Roland's rhetoric and triumphant, we returned to Paris with the precious photocopies in our hands. *Merci mille fois*, Roland.

In Berlin John and I engaged in a disagreeable search of the archives of the Opera House where Laban was choreographer from 1930, in the heart of the Nazi machine. A letter from a Jewish dancer seeking permission to watch a rehearsal was hard to read. Of course she was not permitted but the obsequiousness of her request and the vile wording of its official denial brought home to me the Nazi effect on artists' lives. Letters from parents of the opera's ballet school, closed in the 1932 financial crisis, were redolent with a desire to appease the authorities and reinstate their child. Parents, some Jewish some not, sought to show what good citizens they were, being members of the Party, or participants in the *Kraft durch Freude* (Strength Through Joy) cultural organisation or promising to enrol their son in the Hitler Youth if he were taken back. Profoundly shocked I witnessed how the Jewish parents seemed to have no idea what was coming. They appeared to feel themselves to be just good Berlin citizens.

We studied the archives of the 1936 Olympic Games during which Laban was dismissed. He created the huge movement choir made to open the Games' artistic events. There lay Joseph Goebbels's diary, stating, 'This has nothing to do with us, I forbid it,' written after attending and vetting the dress rehearsal, with Adolf Hitler. There were the notes of Laban's subsequent interrogation by the Gestapo and the savage scribbles made by the Nazi mole placed in his office noting he did not say *Heil Hitler* on arriving each morning. There were the instructions for judging the 1935 International Choreographic Competition.

It must be won by a German company, was the Nazi Party dictate. But Laban, as chairman of the jury, did not comply. Evidence of his response lay in the taxi and shopping receipts where he detailed his secretary to purchase winning gifts for every choreographer. The deadly charade being enacted made difficult reading.

On another occasion I visited Gertrud Snell, Laban's secretary at that time, living in an old people's home in Hanover. I was appalled to find that the dining room was divided in two to separate the residents who had collaborated from those who claimed they had not and this was forty years after the end of the war. I had met Gertrud before at the Art of Movement Studio during my time as a young teacher there. Seeing her later in her own domain in its morass of unforgivingness was something else.

I think it was on the third visit to Vienna that I concentrated on the *fin de siècle* decades when Laban had been enroled by his proud father, General von Laban, as a military cadet for officer training at Wiener Neustadt. In the archives I read of his successes and failures and a note that he had gone AWOL, as indeed he had, desperately, to abandon militarism and start his independent life as an artist in Paris.

Vienna of that period was fascinating to me, an opportunity to discover the Secession, the Viennese version of Parisian Art Nouveau, all evidence of the cultural whirlpool of *fin de siècle* Vienna. The angst of the dying culture in the decades before the First World War were here in the art of Gustav Klimt and Kokoschka, and Secession architecture. On my bedroom wall hangs an Egon Schiele painting of a boy, angular, contorted, reminding me of the hours I spent in the Viennese art galleries and salons, accosted by the evidence of anti-Semitism, the cream cakes, the waltz and the scent of decay. I find Vienna as difficult to stomach as Berlin. Maybe I shouldn't but I do.

John and I visited Laban's son Roland in his modest shooting lodge near Graz. A welcoming man, he was doing his best to understand his father's dramatic life. Roland had never met him, as far as he could remember, just heard rumours. Laban had abandoned family life as soon as WW1 ended, to pursue his obsessive quest for dance, in Germany. He left his wife Maja with five children, Roland being a two year old, as well as his lover Susi with a son, born the same month. By conventional standards both women should have given him the boot but neither did. Convention was never part of their lives or his. He was a man driven by his quest for dance against which domesticity stood no chance.

Thirty years later, when I met him, I fell under his spell as had they, and experienced what it was like to live and work with a man driven beyond comfort, night and day obsessed with what he was writing, making, leading, researching. He called us apprentices his family. We were. Some intimate, others not. Having arrived from a completely conventional family life, his ways were a shock to me, but I relished it. It felt as if I were meant to be there, then, doing that.

Dorothy by a poster for a Fédération Internationale de Danse gathering for which we were both jury members

Leading a workshop at the Lola Rogge School, Hamburg, Rogge being the pre-war director of the Hamburger Bewgungschöre

CHAPTER 19

1987

Kammertanzbühne

As more and more information came to light on Laban's German heritage I took the view that we must somehow reignite interest in Laban's choreographic creativity that appeared to have been radical in the extreme. Had his experiments led to a cul-de-sac, a short-lived wonder, one could have let it lie unrevealed, but what about the well-known choreographers influenced by him? Not only first generation students Wigman and Jooss, but much later William Forsythe and Pina Bausch, both current giants in dance theatre, were influenced by quite different aspects of his work.

What I was finding was new movement, new topics, new use of sound, collaborative rehearsal methods, new training of dancers, technically and creatively, with an emphasis on male dancers. So with much assistance I set about re-finding an evening's-worth of his dances. Over two weeks, in 1987, with student, faculty and guest dancers and percussionists, we made and presented a programme of the Kammertanzbühne Laban 1923-28, works for his modest sized chamber company. The performance attracted an audience and interested criticism in the *Evening Standard*, so a beginning of a long process of rehabilitation had been started.

Rehearsals and show were filmed so that a documentary DVD could record our efforts. The damnable characteristic of dance is that it disappears, literally as you dance it. Unless you get the money not only for the show but for a film all that practical research and innovation would disappear like a sandcastle at high tide. I found a sponsor and the DVD *Laban Dances 1924-28* was the result.

Re-finding some of the dances had happened by chance, *Marotte* was one such. Translated its title means Mad or Demented One. I was visiting Aurel Milloss, his Rome apartment oozing erudition and theatricality, he being a long established and revered European choreographer, latterly in Italy. He recalled having seen a performance of the Kammertanzbühne Laban in 1926 while a ballet student, an experience that changed his life. He remembered *Marotte* performed by Laban as if he had seen it yesterday.

Rising to his unsteady feet he gesticulated a churning motion of his right fist covering his gut, his breathing, repeated again and again, in gasps. Then he flung himself across the room, cried out, then raucously laughed. I rose to my feet alarmed, but he sank slowly to his knees. '*Nella forma del Rondò,*' he said, different 'verses' returning to the churning motif. Calmed, he collected himself and gave me glimpses of other solos and duos, *Orchidée*, the trade mark solo of Dussia Bereska, seated on a dais, bare-breasted exotic vibrating arm movements accompanied by a resonating Chinese bell. He described an 'ecstatic' duo for two priest-like figures in masks and flowing garments and another, a slapstick comedy for two men in grass skirts on male competitiveness, '*Come galli da combattimento*', he said, poking his 'fighting cock' head this way and that and flapping his 'wings' pseudo aggressively.

Back home I could scour the Kammertanz programmes and identify the duos, *Ekstatische Zweimännertanz* and *Bizarre*, both cast for two men. Meetings like this one with Milloss and others with elderly dancers gave me the parameters of the repertoire, extraordinary, unlike anything else.

In 1921-23 Laban had choreographed evening-long works for his Tanzbühne his thirty-strong dance theatre company and I could not attempt to re-find those without the financial resources needed so to do. I concentrated on works for his small company the Kammertanzbühne Laban. His 1935 autobiography recounts how he and his entourage were a resident company in a specially adapted theatre space giving performances several nights a week, quite a choreographic challenge. They had to be financially self supporting so what they offered must attract audiences. A varied programme of comic, beautiful, erotic, awe-inspiring, dramatic dances was what they aimed to provide so we set about trying to do the same, starting with the solos and duos described by Milloss.

The printed programme for our first performances reminds me of one comic quartet. Comedy in dance is never easy but working on *Marsch* I recalled how Laban relished individuality, including the idiosyncrasies of us students. So in *Marsch* I played on the contrasting physiques of four dancers, a very tall slender man, a petite woman and two middle-sized women, one more robustly built than the other. For vocabulary I drew on military formation drill and the scales of movement in his technique that had masculine combative qualities. Danced by this physically incompatible bunch of dancers it engendered laughter so I was encouraged that we had found something near to the original. For the recapitulation the entrance marching was performed by one dancer drooped in 'exhaustion' and a second with a 'goose step' Nazi style and that too worked ironically. One collaborator was a talented musician who researched possible sound accompaniment coming up with a penny whistle improvising on a German army tune. In his biography Laban recounts how penniless they were and how they shared the roles of costume-maker, musician, rehearsal director, choreographer, so we did the same.

Oben und Unten, later renamed *Star Gazer*, had been a popular piece playing on the antics of three astronomers vying with each other as they searched the skies. Their various imagined 'relationships' with the evening star, two comets and the moon made opportunity for all sorts of duos and trios ranging through the emotions of requited and unrequited love. Laban had discussed the work in his autobiography so I had something firm to work from, including his drawing of a figure with telescope looking upwards and the other of the Moon figure.

It was the suite *Die Grünen Clowns* that offered the greatest variety. Photographs from 1927 suggested the movement material, some bizarre, some shocking, some touching. I drew on all my memories of working with Laban to help me make use of the images. *Green Clowns* is the result, referring as it does to Pilkington Tile Works for *Machine*, to his 1948 group study *Chaos Fight and Liberation* for *War*, to close scrutiny of the 1927 photographic images for the *Dying Procession* and *Eccentrics' Club*, and the notation analysis of all kinds of touch and relatedness for *Romance in Green*. While this mish mash of resources might seem a bizarre way of working my research told me that *Green Clowns* first appeared as separate scenes for specific audiences and only appeared as a suite in 1928.

The photographs show that the number of dancers performing differed radically so creativity and adaptation were the norm. Made with Laban's rehearsal methods and editing techniques that I had learnt first-hand, techniques that can be used with any and every cast, *Green Clowns* has been the ideal work to take round the globe and that I and my younger colleagues have done over three decades.

Years later Alison Curtis-Jones became the rehearsal director for the *Clowns'* documentary film. She has gradually and ably taken over my role as re-creator of Laban's oeuvres. For her first rehearsals of *Nacht* I still hovered as artistic adviser but now it is with great pleasure that I can sit back and enjoy seeing where she will take the next.

The process of re-finding, re-creating, re-presenting Laban works has continued, latterly in 2014, at Monte Verita, the so-called Mountain of Truth, in Switzerland, a magical mini-mountain rising on the shore-line of Lake Maggiore. Here Laban's original experiments took place. Recently an art film by Swedish filmmakers had been shown telling the story of the 1900 Mountain of Truth community, a visionary group, avant-garde, anarchic. I had had a minor advisory role in its making and a modest few minutes appearance in it. With that film as a background it seemed the right time to find the very first two dances made in Monte Verita in 1913/4. Re-envisaged creatively by Alison Curtis-Jones, *The Dancing Drumstick* and *Ishtar's Journey into Hades* were performed stupendously by her Summit Dance Theatre. I contributed what an octogenarian should, knowledge, advice when asked but no direct involvement.

The citizens of Lugano were astonished by what they saw and heard as had been their predecessors a hundred years before. After a shocked silence, they gave a standing and vociferous ovation. Nudity, dance with no music but the sound of footfall and breath is not 'Strictly Come Dancing', with its razzmatazz, but somehow profound. The German language uses the word *UR* for things fundamental, *Urtanz*, getting down to the crux of what dance is without glitz and sequins and clever tricks. Luckily the Swiss Arts Council had supported the idea copiously so Curtis-Jones had been able to audition the best artists to work with.

The gut churning in *Marotte*, Philip Forbes in the first re-creations (Ph. Toni Nandi)

Krystall a duet drawing sharp straight lines, Ema Jankovic and Verena
Schneider (Ph. Roswitha Chesher)

Cover for the DVD of the recreations of the *Solos and Duos* suite 2010 (Verve
Publishing & Vitafilms)

Rehearsal shots during the first recreations of the *War* scene in *Green Clowns*
(Ph.Toni Nandi)

Laban's *Die Grünen Clowns* 1928 (Laban Collection)

Alison Curtis-Jones and I consulting with musician Oli Newman on the sound for *Nacht* (Ph. Kyle Stevenson)

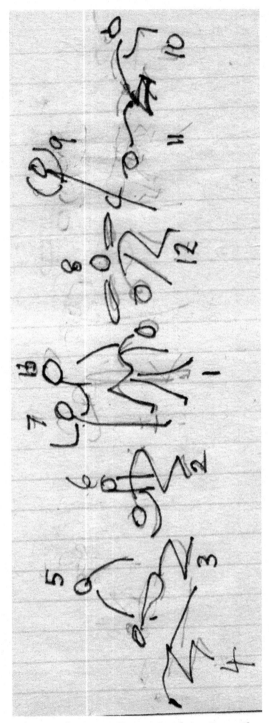

A sketch for the canon in the Dying Procession for a *Green Clowns* performance
for a cast of twelve dancers

Poster for the first perfomances of *Nacht* in 1927 exhibited at Trinity Laban's
International Conference 2008 *Then and Now* (Laban Library)

CHAPTER 20

1988

Re-Finding an Extraordinary Life

Yesterday my U3A German Conversation group met in the local hotel for a celebratory afternoon tea, a meal I never normally eat. Indeed the notion of afternoon tea conjures images of sitting at the table in the nursery with Nanny instructing me in the necessary manners of bread and butter first, then a sandwich and finally a piece of cake, with no licking of fingers, no taking before being invited to take, no getting down from the table mid meal. The group has been an excellent way to keep my German language going now that I don't need it daily as indeed I did over decades.

As the Laban Collection grew and the Kammertanz re-creations began to take shape I could see that publication would have to be the next output. Lisa Ullmann had commissioned John Hodgson, drama academic, to write Laban's life. Hodgson had visited Russian-occupied East Germany ostensibly on a walking tour, actually to locate a house where Laban had hidden his archives when he fled in 1937. Hodgson had found a trunk in a cellar, in the remains of a bombed-out house, looked through the contents and returned with what he could carry in a rucksack, so circumventing the Stazi. It seemed obvious to me that he and I should collaborate sharing our various evidence but that was not Hodgson's plan. He was not for sharing anything. He did allow me to visit his London flat where he brought out from a hiding place single items, a pastel portrait of Dussia Bereska, costume designs for a choreography, but he was not going to show me the bulk of his finds. So what now?

I decided to attempt a book of translations of the journal *Schrifttanz* 1928-32 copies of which John and I had found in an antiquarian bookshop in Nuremberg. That city, decimated in the war, had risen from the ashes as if nothing had occurred. But it had occurred, the ghosts of the notorious and monstrous Nuremberg rally and the trials for war crimes of the Nazi elite in the months after capitulation were imbedded in the foundations of the city. Above, now, stood pristine copies of the mediaeval market place but empty, still unoccupied except for a few brave craftsmen and the bookseller hoping to make a living from the few tourists. But the façade was difficult. You cannot erase monstrosity. The shadow remains.

Schrifttanz was the first attempt in 1928 at an academic journal of dance writings published to coincide with Laban presenting to the dance world his dance notation, his *Tanzschrift*. My German language was not good enough to catch the nuance of the articles so I collaborated with Susanne Lahusen, a native German colleague, and managed to locate Alfred Schlee, the original editor for Universal Edition. By now quite elderly, this erudite Austrian was delighted to write an introduction to *Schrifttanz: A View of Dance in the Weimar Republic*. It received good reviews. We were beginning to give an airing to the material the Nazis had attempted to annihilate.

I thought it worth trying to put together an exhibition hopefully combining the materials and artifacts I had found with Hodgson's. He agreed, hooray. I applied for and achieved a grant and I set about my part of it. Northcote House prepared to publish articles on each section of the exhibition for a catalogue so I began to write and Hodgson promised to join me. In the event his contribution to both text and exhibition was very meagre but to what purpose was unclear. At the top of my stairs is a model torso in white plastic that I used in the exhibition. There it wore Laban's cap and a jacket from a charity shop placed at a table as 'he' wrote a book. On my stairs it changes its clothes according to the weather or my mood. Today 'he' is wearing a Martha's Vineyard sailing cap. Well, why not?

In any event *Rudolf Laban: An Introduction to His Work and Influence* was published. It was about then that I realised that Hodgson had some difficulty with German language. He would clearly have a problem pulling together a comprehensive biography with two thirds of the sources in German. So who would do it? Who was there with the knowledge?

So it was that I set about writing it myself and what a task that proved to be. John agreed to help me, as typist, and we began a combined effort, interspersed with trips across to Europe to fill the gaps in my knowledge. Our last trip together was to Leipzig and en route I knew things were worse for John. But back home all continued apparently well, we were about up to 1924 when John downed tools. No explanation, he simply stood up, left his computer running, my text beside it, went downstairs and that was that. I knew there was no point in discussing what the problem was. He couldn't say, it would only make his sense of failure more poignant. So I continued writing and typing alone.

A year later the text and illustrations were complete, delivered to David Leonard of Dance Books and his marvellous editor Sanjoy Roy. The triumph was that *Rudolf Laban: An Extraordinary Life* was put in for a prize, the American 'de la Torre Bueno Dance Book of the Year', and won it. Champagne! But by myself for John had already gone into his first care home.

Alongside these professional endeavours family life continued as I attempted to be the supportive mother I always hoped I might be and the caring and loving wife I had committed myself 'till death do us part'. I was aware also that my stupid belief that I could accomplish anything took no account of my body or my mental state that reappeared as frail under pressure. Trouble brewed when someone suggested to Marion North that the name Laban was a hindrance to her organisation and it should go. It may well be a hindrance, maybe still is, but it was a shocking thought.

We were at a Laban Centre away weekend gathered to assess progress and plan, or rather they all were, while I flew in from some European country, half way through to hear a stranger round up a presentation proposing the drop of the name. All eyes turned to me for some had hoped that I would stay away and let it happen while others hoped that I would get there in time to fight the corner. I fought. 'What do you want to call it? Bonnie Bird's dance school?' I said. There was an audible intake of breath, Bonnie and Marion turned grey, the man sat down and I walked out of the room unable to control my emotions.

I drove for home, tears streaming down my face, shouting to the ether, 'How dare you!' with probably an expletive, but the weather was icy and snowing a blizzard and I came off the M25 in a slithering zig-zag, shaking but unhurt. A wonderful saviour came to my car window. 'Get back on the road and drive, if you stop to think you won't be able to, so just do it,' he said. I did and got home, just. Still bawling my head off, my daughter wondered what on earth had happened. I could feel my mind and heart and soul in a state of turmoil for I had shocked myself. It brought to the surface what was always there, lurking but controlled, that however I embraced American ideas, European ideas, academic ideas, whatever, my commitment to the man Laban was unbreakable. Assailment of his name was a mortal blow. I wanted my visor to come down, to shield me from... what... I did not know.

With David Leonard and Sanjoy Roy at the Cecil Court bookshop of Dance Books for the launch of *Rudolf Laban: An Extraordinary Life*

With John Hodgson and Marion North, the 'Laban' figure behind in his Don Juan costume in the exhibition *Rudolf Laban: his Work and Influence*

Caught not quite as camera ready as Marion North, Mirella Bartrip newly appointed Vice Principal of the Laban Centre, and Bonnie Bird (Ph. Toni Nandi)

CHAPTER 21

1995

Dance Words

Looking at the monthly schedule for Blackheath Halls, just down the road, all manner of events take place in which one can participate including tea dances, absolutely not my thing, but they recall my time collecting material for *Dance Words*. Harwood Academic Publishers asked me to collate a dictionary on the language current in the dance world, thinking, erroneously, that there might be a concise core of common terms, ways of describing what we do in the studio as we earn our living, variously. But our terminology in the tea dance and the ballet studio is quite specific. So far from a small dictionary it became a collection of phrases recording variety and specificity, from hip hop to Butoh.

Being in New York when the contract came through off I went to the Merce Cunningham Studio to watch a Cunningham technique class and discuss the plan with wonderful dance editor and minder of the Cunningham Foundation, David Vaughan. Question was: what was I listening for? I had to come up with an overall strategy, a way of making order out of a flood of words, a way of sifting studio talk that contained idiosyncrasies that mattered from sheer studio slang, transient ways of getting what you want into the performance. Back to the Guggenheim Museum, cup of Americano and a wet towel.

The dance world is diverse, could I encompass all of it? Bebop, Street, Ballet, Physical Theatre, Contact Improvisation, Tanztheater, Contemporary, Butoh, Ballroom, Modern, Commercial, Line Dancing, Plastique, Robotics, Postmodern, Ritual, Eurocrash, Kathak, and more. I could see that this assignment was going to take me to rehearsal studios, theatres, platforms, churches, bars, halls, sidewalks, lofts, arenas.... and I would meet all and sundry in the dance world, a dance captain, rehearsal director, choreographer, choryphée, hoofer, danseur noble, notator, choreologist, scene designer, stage hand, angel, and more. So back to London to start.

Dance Words was published in 1995, all 718 pages of it. That tells you what a task it was. One enjoyable week was watching Anna Markard, Kurt Jooss's daughter, putting her father's masterpiece *Green Table* on the Birmingham Royal Ballet, listening to how she rehearsed what she needed to achieve to lift the work from Labanotation score to performance. I knew Anna from years back in Essen, at the Folkwang dance department, she a student, me attempting to notate Jooss's new post-war works for the company in the freezing winter of 1951-2. Anna had made it her life's work to remount and preserve her father's repertoire. In Birmingham she had dancers with ballet training, not Jooss technique training, and dancers take into their bodies the style they train in and its way of thinking.

So she had a task, and a sharp rehearsal director she was, organised to the hilt to use every minute she was given to graft the unfamiliar style into their bodies. 'Use the weight of your torso,' 'freeze the leg gesture,' 'where's the peripheral tension?' Here was Jooss terminology and into *Dance Words* it went.

In another studio Judith Maelor Thomas was remounting Ashton's *Symphonic Variations* working from the Benesh notation score, getting the steps and the spacing. 'Use your tram lines', 'don't kill the centre couple', 'work on a shallow diagonal', were what she said to enable the dancers to know how to use the stage space for this ballet. Michael Somes, one of the original cast, rehearsed the performance quality: 'Make it register', 'use your sense of presence', he urged the three male soloists.

Then off to Penge, to the Spencer Dance Centre where I found 'couples strutting their stuff' in Ballroom and Latin. They were not 'partners rehearsing a pas de deux'. Instead of *'pas de basque, assemblé, sissonne'*, it was 'swing, step brush kick, a spot turn'. Whereas Birmingham Royal performed 'in costume and make up', Peggy Spencer's wore their 'outfit and slap'. Peggy had her 'formation team' while Birmingham had their 'corps de ballet'. Two worlds, so different, but in each dedicated dancers sweating it out.

I came to know a bit more about the Ballroom and Latin scene when a new student arrived to study the Master's Degree at the Laban Centre, a champion in the Latin field, and what a breath of fresh air he was. I suppose I was used to students keeping me somewhat at a distance with an element of respect and formality in how I taught and they learnt.

Not so here. 'Come on, darling', he said, 'you know something I want, so spill the beans.' There was nothing aggressive in his demand, just sheer curiosity and desire, but spilling the beans in a way that might enhance competitive Latin was another thing. It gave me cause to think. It pushed me to open out how I was teaching just as it opened him out from showing off his 'stuff' in a standardised way to saying something with his body, expressive, intimate, challenging, all extremely well. But he was a bit of an exploding bomb in class. Wikipedia will tell you that Ruud Vermej has a doctorate and is now a professor so my beans obviously took root.

Preparing *Dance Words* gave me a chance to watch many choreographers at work. One was Christopher Bruce, long associated with Rambert Ballet. He was rehearsing a new piece on his response to Nelson Mandela's emergence from prison, *The Message*. He rehearsed with the set in place, rusty corrugated iron backdrop, a shanty, plus a large black tyre centre stage. You will remember the ghastly images of people in South Africa murdered by having a tyre round their neck, filled with petrol and set alight. That tyre was more than a prop for Kenneth Tharp to move with, it carried overtones of horror that audiences in the 1990s would have recognised. Kenneth slapped, hit, drummed on the corrugated iron scenery making a rhythmic cacophony of intimidating noise. Clearly 'music' was not what he was making but a 'soundscore'.

The print of Schiele's *A Standing Boy* that I have on my bedroom wall reminds me of listening to Lea Anderson creating a work on Egon Schiele, the Viennese expressionist painter. Anderson studied art before she turned to making edgy uncomfortable but riveting choreography. She worked from Schiele's striking and troubled images of the human form. She rehearsed his minutiae, of splayed fingers, a gaze, with the audience's eye in mind. To give each gesture life she found an 'inner narrative' just for one part of the body, 'throw it away,' 'increase the tension in your palm,' or 'more energy in your neck.' It pleased me that the dance analysis language she had encountered while an undergraduate at the Laban Centre stood her in good stead. 'Keep it in the door plane', 'hold the bound flow'.

The piece opened in Bologna, entitled *The Sketchbooks of Egon Schiele*, catching his contorted images, performed by her all-male company The Featherstonehaughs. As it happened I was concurrently giving workshops at Bologna University so witnessed the premiere. As 'a set' she transformed the stage space as an artist's canvas outlined by 'foot lights' and 'fluorescent strips', creating a 'soundtrack' by the scratching of charcoal on paper.

Back in London I visited the home of Yolanda Sonnabend, another visually edgy woman, a frequent designer for Kenneth MacMillan's psychological ballets at Covent Garden. Always looking for fresh images, 'Why not dress them in paper bags?' she suggested. Her home was awash with objects in dark dimly-lit corridors, fragments and debris of her work, 'a model' of a set, 'a mock up' for a costume, 'masks', a decorated mirror, faded flowers, a painted 'body stocking', scraps of fabric. Her creativity was phenomenal but I came away wondering if I had been in a madhouse. Her madness was, of course, what made her work so compelling.

I could not help thinking back to 1952 when making costumes at the Mercury Theatre, the minute theatre in Notting Hill where Ballet Workshop functioned on a Sunday evening, a place for aspiring choreographers to try out new work, make mistakes, learn. MacMillan was there, not yet as a choreographer but trying his hand as a designer. The piece I remember that caused us such grief was Michael Holmes's comedy based on Lear's *The Dong with the Luminous Nose* who 'went to sea in a sieve'. Making costumes that were sieves was a challenge. I can't remember how Nan Austin and I solved it but I do remember the fatigue. We literally fell asleep sitting at our sewing machines in an all-night session, heads flopped on the black metal, my nose an inch from a very sharp needle.

In contrast to Yolanda, Nicholas Georgiadis's language was thoroughly pragmatic. I tracked him down in the corridors of the Royal Opera House. He discussed the first decisions to be made for designing a ballet's set. Will he make it 'a location' that tells a story or abstract, 'a psychological place'. That for him was 'the primary definition' decided between choreographer and designer. For his *Romeo and Juliet* it was definitely 'location', Verona. He was much concerned with the logistics of a rapid scene change as Romeo ran from a luxurious palace to a 'bleak empty space' that somehow 'the crew' had to achieve in an exact number of seconds. The sheer practicalities were part of his trade. His 1:25 models, with architectural drawings in elevation and ground plan, were meticulous.

At Trinity Laban we have a fabulous state-of-the-art theatre, equipped with everything, and a crew capable of giving you just what your designer wants, Georgiadis or whoever. I thought back to my stint as a stage manager with 'The Young Dancers', a trio, a rather different scenario to Covent Garden or Trinity Laban. I think I was eighteen. We were touring Galloway, a rural Scottish county with no theatres but all manner of halls that I was supposed to turn into 'performance spaces'. In one we borrowed sheets from the local inn and pinned them up as 'wings', in another we borrowed straw bales and covered them in brown cardboard. For lights the local grocery loaned us cubic biscuit boxes made of metal into which somehow our lights were screwed with the 'colour gells' resting on top. I think Health and Safety would have had something to say.

While still compiling *Dance Words*, the biography *Rudolf Laban: An Extraordinary Life* was with David Leonard at Dance Books with the editing process in full swing. Finally, with David and editor Sanjoy Roy, we completed all the permissions, the index and bibliography, the illustrations, for its publication date in 1998. Concurrently the Dutch Arts Council asked for a book on dance making. I saw how I could make use in that text of the research for *Dance Words*, an utterly useful process that had widened my knowledge of what was out there and the possible directions that young choreographers might take. Having access to so many dance people at the top of their game educated me in a way that only hands-on experience can, that academic study never could and that a critic's view of the end product cannot. That and the experience of mentoring at the Fédération Internationale de Danse led to *Looking at Dances: a choreological perspective on choreography*.

I wrote *Looking at Dances* at Aldeburgh, sitting under a copper beech tree, supplied with white wine and homemade fruitcake by the intrigued B&B owner. With Dorothy Madden beside me I experimented with how to write a book that was not a textbook but an inspirational book on the act of choreographing. Just as *A Handbook for Modern Educational Dance* had been in its day I wanted *Looking at Dances* to be thoroughly practical, a book to take with you into the studio and open there and then. So I wrote it as I speak in the studio, as I had heard Dorothy speak, as I had heard so many choreographers speak, not how one talks in the lecture theatre, but through short sentences, questions, designed to enable readers to think for themselves.

The text offered concepts on the bricks and mortar of making a theatre work and of enabling it to reach spectators in the way the choreographer wanted. Back in London I commissioned an artist to sketch six dancers in action and 'choreographed' the drawings into the text. The rough copy looked like a page of poetry. It was not, but it gave that impression. No publisher would touch it, so I set up my own publishing company for I was not for altering the concept. That was how that book had to be.

Thinking back to 1960, before the time of computers, keyboarding or cut and paste, holding the badly typed copy of my first book, the *Handbook*, clutched to my chest, I had advanced with false confidence to John Street, to meet John Macdonald, of Macdonald and Evans, publishers. There he sat, a robust character, behind an impressive desk close to an equally impressive wine cabinet, or rather gin cabinet. I made several visits, for John Macdonald enjoyed giving his writers a tough time but also a liquid time. My liver was seriously taxed by publication date. I learnt a good deal about publishing from John Macdonald, the mechanics of turning copy into book, writing for your reader, the value of your editor and designer, sorting your marketing plans. It all stood me in good stead when, almost forty years later, I set up Verve Publishing.

Having written several books by then I knew what I wanted to say and how I wanted to say it and whom I hoped to reach through it. I knew what sort of books would sit on a library shelf read only by postgraduates, mine included, and what sort would be dog-eared with use, stuffed into a workbag and be taken into a studio for daily scanning. I hoped *Looking at Dances* would be the latter. It was the first Verve publication, with Glenn Hilling as designer.

I seem to collaborate with people who live in houses that are in transition. Glenn clearly was turning a routine semi into a ravishing modern home but he also enjoyed designing, playing with his son, et al, et al, et al. Somehow each time I achieved Enfield after a hazardous drive on the North Circular I felt a hard hat would be the wisest headgear as I climbed to the top floor up a staircase resembling a precipice. Once up in Glenn's design studio, every sort of modern device was pristinely in place with *Looking at Dances* beginning to take shape, expertly.

Dance is a Language isn't it had been my first effort at choreographing a book and there it still is, thirty-five years later, still being read, still in its first amateur state, typed, as I recall, in a caravan on holiday with my children. My life's concern has been to integrate the theory and the practice of dance so of course I have to choreograph the pages as if each were a performance space. *Dance is a Language* is crude, all that typing, Tippex, pen and ruler could do. What Glenn did for *Looking at Dances* was a work of artistic vision as he composed each page with font, borders, print size, colour and placed the drawings, horizontal, right angled, inverted, in the wings...

Looking at Dances took off as a marketing exercise, torrentially. My study became a postal sorting office, and continued every fall, year on year. On its fourth printing I passed it on to Dance Books. After twenty years it is still selling although it is said that people hardly buy books any more. They expect to find everything instantaneously on the Internet.

Dance and the Performative (2004) I wrote with dance theatre artist Ana Sanchez Colberg. Although Ana was a reluctant writer and I had to drag copy out of her, I needed her. In the ten years since *Dance Words,* the arts world had moved on, postmodern was old hat and post postmodern was where we were, or where Ana was. This book had to accommodate to that change. While *Looking at Dances* was a practical book for student choreographers few people had written for the postgraduate choreographer. But Master's degrees in Choreography existed. What I attempted, with Ana, was an amalgam of studio practice with academic concepts, concepts from theatre studies, phenomenology, semiotics, proprioception, all those things that we both knew but that can alienate a practitioner on first sight.

I knew this text would not be a best-seller but I wanted to reach that smaller market. So back to Glenn Hilling to try to soften the academic blow by inserting images. I love what he did, the use of black pages and white, dancers emerging from text. But not all reviewers in the UK agreed. Too fanciful for academics, too heady for practitioners. However, I have to say it amused me that a Trinity Laban colleague taking an MFA in a USA university found *Dance and the Performative* his prescribed text. Like *Looking* I passed it on to David Leonard of Dance Books for its later printing.

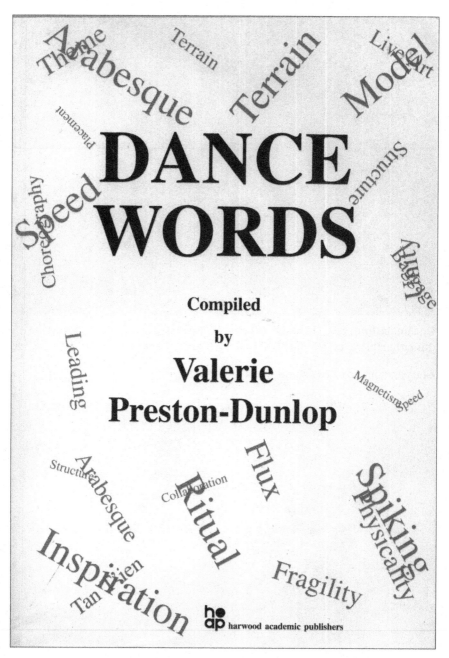

Title page of *Dance Words*

One image from Lea Anderson's *The Sketchbooks of Egon Schiele* showing the 'inner narrative' in action (Ph. Pau Ross, Courtesy Lea Anderson)

One page spread of *Looking at Dances*

CHAPTER 22

1997

Long Haul

The ease with which we in the UK can pop into a café or buy groceries, as I have done this morning in the row of independently-owned shops in Greenwich, is in sharp contrast to the situation in Moscow in 1997 soon after glasnost. Transitions Dance Company were invited to attend the first international dance festival run by Russia since the Berlin Wall came down, held in Volgograd, erstwhile Stalingrad. One of their pieces was Laban's *Green Clowns* and I was detailed to travel with them along with the company's director Bill Cratty.

What an event, starting with what a journey. We flew into Moscow to find ourselves in a student housing block of the utmost frugality, alive with every sort of livestock you can imagine, especially in the shower rooms. No such thing as en suite, no convenient tray for tea in the room or minibar, nothing. Worse, there appeared to be no such thing as a café in house or in the streets, so supper? No corner shop to buy in something edible? We went to bed hungry. In the morning, having recovered from a visit to the vermin infested bathroom, and avoided the cockroaches underfoot, a courier led us miles across Moscow to a prearranged early-morning breakfast and on to Moscow railway station to board the train for the overnight trip south.

Bill and I were together in a somewhat modest first-class sleeper while the twelve dancers were in six-berth standard class, scattered across the train, sharing with a contingent of unwashed Russian soldiers, merry and apparently on leave who regarded the dancers as their good fortune. Bill and I set up a twenty-four hour watch as the last thing we wanted was a company of dancers exhausted from continuous self-defence against the amorous militia.

Bill already knew he had cancer, this was his last trip, his last assignment. Between duties up and down the carriages he shared with me his hopes and fears. By his death a year later he had planned his funeral. 'I want to go out in a performance.' He did, with a hearse drawn by four black-plumed horses and top-hatted grooms.

Volgograd itself, a city risen like a phoenix out of the ashes of its WW2 catastrophe, was equally short on any of the facilities that we regard as normal, even essential. Impressive new-build open spaces, prestigious monuments but no shops, cafés or bars. We were escorted everywhere, again miles across an almost empty city for institutional food. At least it made the dancers feel that London was heaven on earth compared with the austerity here. The company made a good impression and the trip was certainly an education for all. The return journey was by plane to Moscow in a transport, where we sat on the floor, alongside crates of whatever, one knew not what. I was glad to get home in one piece.

But home was empty. With John now in care, permanently forty miles from Ightham, Emma ensconced in a flat in London and Roger plus Venetia in Berkshire there was no point in remaining in Corners with its three staircases, four bathrooms, four 'reception' rooms, me and the cats. I had tried dividing it back into what it originally was, a house with cottages attached, and let the cottage part, but I couldn't bear it, the visual impact of the house just gone. So back to my birthplace I came, buying again in Blackheath.

I already owned one flat with Dorothy living there when not on her French forays or her annual two months back in Martha's Vineyard, New York, Washington. Her friendship was increasingly important to me as John diminished. I needed someone to come back to, to drink a glass of wine with, to discuss, to care about. We would meet in France wherever she had been mentoring and take off to places we were interested in.

Montaillou was one, the ruined mediaeval village in the Cathar countryside, home of sheep farmers, whose forebears, in the twelfth century, had been unpleasantly interrogated for their religious beliefs. Here were shepherds undertaking the same annual transhumance with their decorated flocks from winter homestead to the grazing grounds of the Montaillou hills. The only modernity seemed to be their jeans.

For another we followed in the footsteps of Robert Louis Stevenson and his *Travels with a Donkey*, finding the very chestnut groves and rivers he described. As Dorothy aged, she was eighteen years my senior, she eventually admitted frailty. Being an ace driver on the right, she loved the freedom of French roads, as she did the highways of Washington or the byways of Martha's Vineyard. But after one perilous angina episode driving on the zig-zag Cevennes Corniche, she reluctantly relinquished the wheel. Then it was usually back to England for me to continue professional opportunities while she took off for America.

Japan was to be my next long-haul venue, to a conference on German Expressionism. I never understood why the Japanese came to have such an affinity with German culture. During the 1920s Laban had been decorated with a Japanese award, but why? In the 1970s my 1963 book had been translated into Japanese by a professor. Madam Matsumoto came to Beechmont with hands pressed together, bowing to John and me, as we discussed the niceties of creative dance, in a behavioural ritual. It seemed to me so odd that the freedom of the creative ideas espoused in the text was being taken to a country still riven with conventions, but it was. The first Physical Education College for Women opened in Tokyo in 1967, with dance, so I suppose my book was their text for a few years.

The Tokyo invitation was a chance to give Emma a glimpse of the other side of the globe as I had done earlier for Roger to Australia, so off we went together. I thought this would be a great opportunity to see old Japanese culture so we were booked into a traditional ryokan and that was a horrible mistake. The room was bare, one was expected to sit on the floor, on tatami mats, while after a long flight I was longing for a soft bed and comfortable rest. No such thing, the only 'furniture' being a telephone on the floor. The bathroom was a traditional communal one. Emma was fine with it all but I was not, so after one night and breakfast sitting crossed legs we moved to a modern hotel. Hooray.

The conference had scheduled workshops on *Green Clowns* for Keio University students, dance students I presumed. But no, they were male Physical Education students, brawny young sports-playing men. Ah. I guessed that the *War* scene would be most appropriate to start with and it was. They were brilliantly athletic, the thrusts and lifts and falls and shouts were phenomenal. With no women among them I saw that the *Romance* scene was problematic. I had no idea, and was not prepared to find out, how they would take to the rudeness and blasphemous material in *Eccentrics' Club* so *Machine*, the conveyor belt section, was what we tried next. The scene is a metaphor for machine dominating man in the

industrial 1920s culture. It requires an uncomfortable unison exactness that our own dancers find unpleasant. These young men got it brilliantly, obeying orders being part of their culture. So the two-scene version of Japanese *Green Clowns* was a virtuosic blockbuster lacking the pathos of the original but I believe Laban would have relished it.

I wish I could say that I loved the Japanese gardens, the pagodas, the manicured trees, but while I admired them I found them difficult, alien. My relationship with nature is one of mutuality, I nurture plants and wild life, doing my best to allow them to flourish and blossom in their own way. Here nature was tamed, silent, clipped and 'bonsaied', controlled into a beautiful object, while what I liked and shared was nature's physicality, albeit untidy, with birdsong.

We were invited to a Kabuki performance, and skillful it was but horribly bloody. Having embraced Quakerism, with its commitment to nonviolence, I am not good at people striking each other and generally being savage. So I concentrated on the skill and the colours and the tradition as my best coping strategy. I love Japanese Butoh performance, its tenderness and care are such a contrast. As a small person, on the beach at Selsey, our place for family summer holidays, once a week the Punch and Judy man set up his stall. The story is vicious. It frightened me horribly. I could not bear it. I wept bitterly and clung to Nanny. The same feeling of revulsion came over me with the Kabuki show. Violence and me do not go together, and yet I can rehearse the *War* scene in *Green Clowns*. How absurd is that?

In our hotel in Kyoto we nearly came to grief for we were not used to the house rules. Emma and I were all for trying the communal bathing expected so down we went, she wrapped in a towel, I in a swimsuit. There we found women, naked, in small clusters, undertaking their pre-bath ablutions. The look they gave me for my swimsuit was withering, so off it had to come. I have to say I am not good at nudity in public, my not-so-young body is not pretty but then looking around, nor were theirs. This hotel being somewhat up-market the women tended to be well fed, some roundly plump, not to say fat, so I relaxed and advanced to join Emma in the huge communal tub. The women's withering looks continued but focused on Emma. Then I read the notice on the wall, 'No Tattoos Permitted'. As a fact Emma has tattoos, one of which on her right buttock is in Chinese. Luckily it is neither rude nor blasphemous, but she did cover herself and, smiling and bowing a polite goodbye, we thought it best to beat a retreat.

The next year I was back in South America, in Rio de Janiero, my first visit being with John, staying in the Hilton as a Patent Attorney's wife. Immediately outside the front door of that hotel had been a *favella*, literally right there. The contrast of the opulence within with the squalor and poverty without was awful. It was perhaps the first time that I had smelt deep poverty close up. Our Beechmont clubs for people in need looked like a palatial tea party compared with this.

Walking in Greenwich Park this week the squawking parakeets that fly there, with their wonderful turquoise feathers, reminded me of the exoticism of Rio. What took me there this time was an international conference, a celebration for transatlantic work influenced by Laban's broad innovations, organised by the New York based Laban/Bartenieff Institute for Movement Studies (LIMS). I was invited to give the keynote and presented a workshop, again on *Green Clowns*. The piece draws you in because the movement material is odd, intriguing, but easy to read. This was *Green Clowns* first outing to South America, albeit a workshop performance, and it caused considerable interest.

LIMS curriculum does not include anything on Laban's theatre work, nor should it, their brief being the study of behaviour patterns. Notwithstanding that difference, about this time LIMS kindly gave me a lifetime award. It took the form of a lemniscate beautifully crafted from wood and it sits beside the de la Torre glass tablet given me for Laban's biography. So thank you New York.

I walked down the Copacabana beach, drove through the Tijuca rainforest. Up I climbed to the Christ Redeemer figure towering above the city, all of which I had done before, with John. And there he was now in Drake Court Care Home, lying on his bed. I liked to believe he might be thinking of me as I was of him, but I knew it was not so. His world had contracted to those uncomplicated things he could cope with. Once, sitting on his bed after a walk together, I asked him what he thought about. His answer was simple, just one word, 'Breakfast'. So any thought that I and the family might be in his mind was knocked on the head. I asked him once if he would like me to visit more than once a week such was my fantasy that I was still important to him. Without a hesitation, 'No', he said. The Maidstone hospital consultant had probably been right when he advised, 'Let him go.' Truth was maybe I needed the connection with him more than he needed me.

When John died people were very kind as they are. They spoke about bereavement. It was then that I recognised that I had been in a state of continual bereavement since that fateful Christmas Day, twenty-eight years earlier, the birth of his illness. It is fearful to gradually, slowly, inexorably, visibly, lose the man you love.

This South American trip ended in São Paulo, the sprawling industrial city with its 'teeming masses' and 'disheartening crime and poverty'. I was to give workshops here at Caleidos, the go-ahead creative arts centre, and discovered that Laban's ideas had migrated there from Germany in the 1930s. Not a comfortable city to walk around in, I was advised simply not to. My lasting memory is the river Tiete, an open sewer running through the lower town with floating foam from the industrial waste upstream, a steamy gas hovering over it. At least the Thames has been cleared up, fish survive, cormorants thrive. I was not sorry to get safely home, home by now being Blackheath.

The somewhat bleak port of Volgograd announcing the dance festival

The lemniscate gift from Laban/Bartenieff Institute of Movement Studies, New York, for lifetime service to the work of Rudolf Laban

A glass of wine with Dorothy Madden on return from one of my trips

CHAPTER 23

2004

DVDs in variety

Caroline Lamb visited a few years ago to show me her DVD *Footfalls*, her dance for film, made with 'the older dancer', a less-than-usual casting at that time. I met Caroline during the filming of the documentary *The American Invasion*. Dorothy had been seminal in bringing over American Modern Dance to the UK through courses at Dartington Hall, off and on from 1962 to '72. Caroline had been one of the Dartington students. One summer a confrontation took place between teachers of creative dance, UK, and Dorothy's presentation of dance as a technique-based art form, USA, more or less Martha Graham meets Rudolf Laban, an uncomfortable thought. Through the documentary I set out to capture that impactful summer.

Seeing how people cope with things new is always educative. Here the new was threatening to some, literally threatening their belief system. The current credo in the 1950s and '60s was that creativity was the best form of education. Creative movement practice, whether as dance or drama, was seen as an ideal mode, was indeed a basic human activity available, natural to every child, boy or girl. Coming from over the pond was dance as something else, an art form, female dominated, beautiful but you were not likely to succeed if your body were of the wrong sort, lumpy, too tall, and requiring skills not easily acquired by boys or desirable to them.

Technique-driven dance married with the current change in educational strategies, shifting as it was from training teachers in child-centred methods to subject-centred methods, through acquiring knowledge of dance rather than of children. The government aim was to create a subject degree-based teaching profession rather than enabling people to specialise in children's development, needs and aspirations first and apply their knowledge to a subject second.

The students on Dorothy's course at Dartington were all dance teachers, most of them in responsible positions in training colleges. For the film my aim was to gather people involved in this confrontation, set up interviewing questions and tease out their responses. To change or not to change, that was the issue. At almost ninety Dorothy was just able to take part in filming and determined so to do. I dragged her out of hospital after one of her several angina episodes, and propped her up in her chair to face Luis España's camera.

The juxtaposition in the film of footage of Martha Graham as a dance icon in a theatre, her dancers visible as beautiful, skilful, slender, powerful technicians, contrasted with footage of primary-school-aged young people engaged in spontaneous performance both in dance and word, delicate, collaborative, coming from the heart and soul of the children. I had to show the viewer both and the forty-five second Graham footage cost me many dollars. David Leonard of Dance Books who marketed the video was kind enough to promote it as 'a film every teacher of dance should see' so thank you Luis España and the participants.

That was Dorothy's last public appearance before she went into a nursing home as her angina took hold. Visiting her and John became my regular routine. Thanksgiving Day was still celebrated, her mid-Atlantic frame of mind insisted, turkey (sandwiches), pumpkin pie and champagne were produced to her bedside whereupon she had an inevitable angina episode plus morphine. But heyho, so far as she was concerned, while there was life then live it, and take the consequences.

A few years before in 2001, decidedly elderly, she had made her last trip back 'home'. No longer permitted to fly long-haul she booked on the liner Queen Elizabeth. It was September and she was en route to receive an honour at Maryland University, due to dock in New York, be met and driven south in style. But mid-Atlantic, the awful 9/11 atrocities occurred. New York harbours were closed, the QE2 was diverted to Boston. Suffice it to say she was transported, shaken, to Maryland by a series of buses, received her award and returned to her own home in Martha's Vineyard, in shock.

Her home was a typical Martha's Vineyard white and grey New England cottage, the de rigueur style on the island, enforced and beautiful, primarily summer homes. I had visited the island on several occasions, once taking a 4-seater plane from New York's La Guardia to the modest runway mid-island, a thirty-minute roller coaster ride with the pilot dipping down to glimpse a baseball match en route. We had had a holiday there as a family, when the children were school age, staying in the adjacent cottage owned by Dorothy's adopted sister and her millionaire husband. It was usually inhabited by the pilots of their private plane but we were offered the cottage for a month.

Parts of the island's waters and Edgartown are where you find the rich, in sailing gear, go up island and you see at a distance the very rich living in their protected ranches. Go to the east coast and there is the delightful unspoilt fishing harbour, Menemsha, where you can buy lobster and clams. Oak Bluffs, Dorothy's bit of the island, is unsophisticated, a place to saunter, swim in the sea, rock on the porch and drink a vodka tonic, listening to jazz. But don't come here in the winter. Holidaymakers gone, shops shut, the small resident community gathers and shares its conservative mentality. Half of Dorothy would have loved to live here but as the fall season took hold she knew she could not. So back to England.

The following year Dorothy reached ninety and she being fond of birthdays we celebrated in Bellagio, in a hotel on Lake Como, well known to us both. On the morning of the great day Madame brought up champagne with breakfast, not a bottle but a magnum! 'For old times', she said. Roger and Emma had organised flowers, in quantity, so luxury it was. Then, in sharp contrast, we spent a happy day studying a text by a Quaker, a biochemist working in Geneva, that showed the DNA of a fruit fly to be 85% similar to the DNA of you and I. Really? It caused me to think. The writer also argued that if the world community were to carry on as we were, wrecking the planet through allowing global warming, we, and the fruit fly, would come to grief. It was a beautifully crafted and thought-provoking piece of writing. I returned home a confirmed eco warrior and set up a group to promote climate change responsibility and care for nature.

I believe this was the moment I started a veg patch, behind the garages. This morning I harvested purple-sprouting broccoli, yesterday it was spinach, plus chives for a salad and mint for the homegrown potatoes with strawberries from last summer's crop stored in the freezer.

About this time I succeeded in getting sponsorship to start an advanced course focusing on a contemporary development of choreological praxis.

Getting anything going costs money before it is economic. I knew I could never get the course launched without funds. It was Roger who gave me the argument to put to a sponsor. 'Try this', he said. Aim: a self-sufficient golf course starting from a few acres of grassland. Mr A buys the land, puts in place the hazards and the putting greens while earning nothing so, in debt, has to sell. Mr B buys the course and sets about putting in the infrastructure and the clubhouse while earning nothing so, in debt, has to sell. Mr C buys the course complete, ready to open and runs a successful self-sufficient club. The sponsor was of a sporty disposition, he understood the metaphor, and agreed to cover the costs of the equivalent of Mr A and Mr B.

With this help the Advanced Diploma in Choreological Studies was set up giving us two years to fast track a handful of promising young professionals, recruit internationally and test whether we could break even. We did. It is a flourishing course, led by my colleague Rosemary Brandt, very demanding, and developing future leaders so I begin to feel I can stand back and let the next generation take over.

One aspect of Laban's work I hesitated to publish, choreosophy or the hidden wisdom in dance. I thought hard before making a film on this esoteric aspect of his theories as he had kept it close to his chest in his lifetime, well aware that mention of esotericism makes many people take fright including those in authority in education and academia. He chose to share something of these ideas with a handful of us. Collaborating with Anna Carlisle, a colleague open to the material, we rehearsed dancers and spoke to camera to make the DVD *Living Architecture: Rudolf Laban and the Geometry of Dance*, illustrated by beautiful harmonic movement.

For many thinkers of the turn of the 19th/20th century, spirituality was of interest. In a post-Nietzsche 'God is Dead' culture, with Theosophy and Anthroposophy prevalent and a return to Neo-Platonism in the air, Rosicrucianism re-emerged. Laban, as a student in Paris, along with plenty of other creators including artists Gustav Moreau, Claude Debussy, Erik Satie, Henri Matisse, embraced its cult of perfection and harmony. The DVD gave me the opportunity to bring in specialists well versed in Rosicrucianism to explain to camera these central tenets while Anna and I got on with making beautiful movement on geometric harmonies, rehearsed with the dancers as illustrations of Laban's *Rose Croix* thinking. I had no idea if it would sell at all but it has, a small but devoted market that reignites each year, so someone somewhere is interested enough to be spreading the ideas.

While this DVD was in the making my research with William Forsythe began. Forsythe, choreographer in Frankfurt Opera House, had, as I have earlier described, been blown away by Laban's idea of dance as living architecture. That perspective enabled him to see his beloved heritage, ballet, in a completely new way, not as steps and positions but as moving geometric forms made by the dancer. Trinity Laban applied for and won an Arts and Humanities Research Council award to find a new way of recording how he made his astounding ballets.

His acclaimed multi-media dance theatre pieces, include dance of course, but also video clips, electronic sound, dancers speaking, arguing, whispering and in *The Loss of Small Detail*, snow falling, a thunderstorm and paper strewn all over the stage. What I had to find was a contemporary method that could integrate all those elements in a way that a traditional written text, plus photographs, with a film attached, cannot. That meant a digital, computer-based method. Forsythe donated the archives of *Loss* to Trinity Laban and I set about collaborating with Plymouth University's award-winning IT department and Ana Catalina Roman, the Forsythe company dancer who knew the piece inside out. The grant enabled me to employ technical assistance but it pleased me that I was designing state of the art techie stuff, at my age. The resulting programme consists in twenty-eight interactive 'maps' that enable the user to choose where to start, what to look at, to click up a dance clip or a sound clip or an interview clip from a coherent whole.

Both the *Loss* Project and the *Living Architecture* DVD were complete in time for the 2008 International Conference organised by Trinity Laban to celebrate fifty years of development since Laban's death in 1958. What a contrast in mood and content it was to the centenary. Participants were interested to hear and see each other's developments. With copious events on site, a week-long summer school at Dartington Hall and a performance by Transitions Dance Company in Manchester of the Kammertanz re-creations, through a wonderful team led by Lesley Ann Sayers we did the man proud.

Alongside all these commitments and innovations I visited John, on Sundays, Dorothy every free evening. It was John who weakened first, failing, falling and ending in Lewisham Hospital. He was patched up but it was all too much for him and I could see that he was fading. His last ten days were in the same nursing home as Dorothy. He died peacefully with Emma and I and Dorothy beside him. We just missed our golden wedding day by four weeks.

We celebrated his life by hiring a River Thames boat, with forty people coming from every stage of his life from a school friend, Beechmont friend, godchild, grandchildren, to his last carer from Drake Court. We enjoyed a cream tea, his favourite meal, as we sailed up the Thames.

Before the year was out Dorothy died, not calmly but with a final battle to free herself from her troublesome body. With no family of her own it was her adopted Dunlop family that laid her to rest in a quiet Quaker service. John's and Dorothy's ashes were buried side by side, with room for mine in between.

The Director of Trinity Laban Anthony Bowne escorting me after delivering the keynote at the 2008 *Then and Now* conference

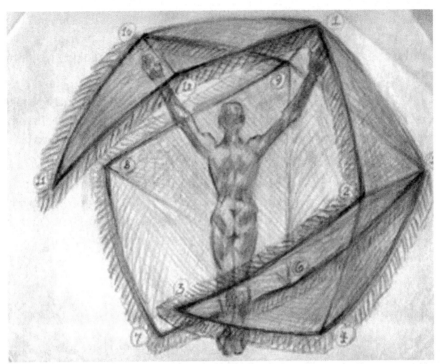

One of Laban's drawings illustrating his Rosicrucian perspective on choreosophy (Laban Collection)

Amanda Banks and Johan Stjerholm demonstrating from the DVD *Living Architecture* at the conference

With Anna Carlisle at a presentation of the DVD *Living Architecture* at Monte Verita (Ph. Paolo Tosi)

Presenting the Loss Project at the *Then and Now* conference with Forsythe dancer Ana Catalina Roman

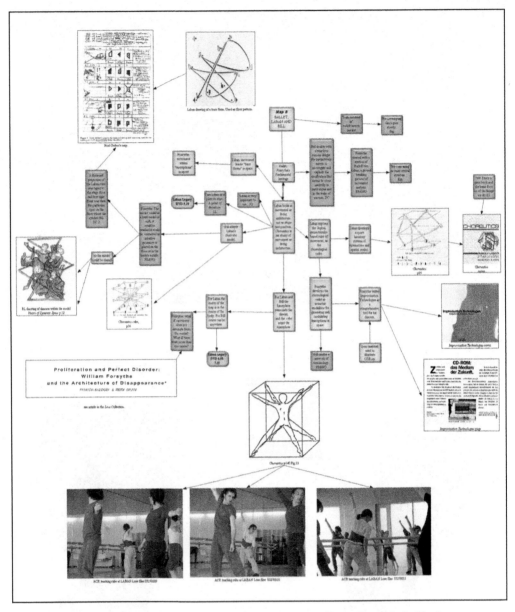

One interactive page from the research project on William Forsythe's *The Loss of Small Detail*

CHAPTER 24

2014

A Second Look and In Memoriam

The year 2014 being the centenary of World War One my mind turned to the mud of Flanders and the trenches of the Somme. My father, Bill, had been a padre attached to the Liverpool Pals when the disastrous battle of the Somme opened on July 1st 1916. Trones Wood was where he offered the wine and bread to the men before their attack, a battle which so few survived. I wanted to make a memorial work, a movement choir for all ages, for war affects everyone not only those in the hellish mêlée.

To refresh my mind I revisited the battlegrounds closest to our family. I wept in the cemeteries at Trones Wood and Passchendaele reading name after name of young man who had lost his life, in terrible waste. Frank's body is not there, he was never found, just shot and swallowed up by the Flanders quagmire. We found 'Capt. Francis Ward' remembered at the awesome Tyne Cot cemetery with its memorial for the thousands of fallen with no grave. Will we ever learn?

On return I commissioned *In Memoriam 2014*, featuring all ages, an hour-long creative movement choir for the memorial year to WW1. Fifty undergraduates formed the bulk of the performers with the nine-year-old boys and girls from a local primary school, and the Retired But Not Tired group of over-sixties men and women dancers. Five brass players, a four-part choir plus a percussionist made the sound score along with traffic and aeroplane noise. Was I mad to attempt such a mammoth project? Probably, but I had several rehearsal directors to help me.

The whole event was performed for filming outside on the sculpted grass hillocks that comprise the campus round the ultramodern Laban building. The surrounding context expresses what the piece was about, destruction and hope, worn-out industrial buildings being torn down juxtaposed with new high-rise flats. The Laban building itself is a metaphor for hope and renewal for it was built on the abandoned rubbish tip of Lewisham borough, cleansed and reformed as a landscaped performance venue adjacent to the working river Thames.

Roswitha Chesher, the marvellously collaborative film director appointed to shoot and edit the action, was adept at sprawling on wet grass, kneeling, any action of her body, to get the best shot, the telling moments, when, in the war scene, dancers leap, crash, shout, hit and snarl, or when the children peer over the hilltops and witness the 'dying people', or when 'the seniors' gather to venerate the 'war memorials'. The piece ended with the whole company clustering in multi-age groups for farewell and departure as the choir sang a pianissimo prayer on the hope of love.

Filming is always tedious, waiting about to be called, repeating shots over and over. The undergraduates are prepared and used to the tedium of filming, their patience and readiness is all part of their training. But you can imagine the logistics over two days of harnessing twenty-five small people clad in white leggings and tops with bells on their ankles ready and waiting and excited to do the bit they had created, dodging the showers, beside twenty senior citizens, clad in silver and grey, nervously anticipating how to transfer their material, rehearsed in a studio, to an outdoor open arena, quite disorientating and muscle-memory interrupting.

Creating stuff takes money that in the past would have been an investment cost that with good advertising, could be repaid from sales. Not now. When it came to publishing *In Memoriam 2014* much of it went straight on to the Internet for that is where the young search, not in bookshops or even DVD shops on line. They expect to get their information free by downloading it. Luckily I was able to find a sponsor for the performance and filming but the Internet is a colossal problem for publishing.

A few months later I was performing myself, not for film but live at Blackheath Halls. I entered through the stage door, costumes over my shoulder, preceded by three dancers, en route to the newly refurbished Recital Room. We were there for a run-through for a public presentation. The last time I used this entrance was as a somewhat rusty alto for a performance of Brahms' *Requiem* with the Blackheath Choir where I gave the *Laudate Dominum* and *Agnus Dei* my best and loved it. The time before was almost eighty years ago as a small person taking part in a Christmas pantomime, in which one I cannot recall but being four I had a seriously insignificant role, possibly a rabbit in *Babes in the Wood*, or a lamb in a Nativity scene. Nanny, of course, would have been in attendance.

The present endeavour was to guide the public into how to look at contemporary dance and really enjoy the process. Tony Brewer who invited me to take on the task had said, somewhat challengingly, why not call the event 'Why Bother?' His experience of contemporary dance had clearly been unrewarding and he is not alone. Contemporary dance performances can be opaque. Our aim was to open the genie's bottle and reveal what there is to be seen and give the spectators some tools to look with.

Dance is never a straightforward art form for lecture demonstrations. Music is easier. No need to memorise examples, just find a musician, get hold of a score and a music stand and your demonstration material is half-way there. Not so for dance, you can only demonstrate what is stored in the dancers' bodies, in their muscle memory, you can't produce a score and say: 'Please dance this now.'

We wanted to share with the spectators an insider view of how choreographers think, starting with Merce Cunningham's methods, showing how he made his movement choices using chance procedures, to avoid the ordinary, to find the unusual. He threw dice to decide right or left, turn or jump, three steps or four, arm or no arm. We wanted to share William Forsythe's method of using geometric spatial forms starting by joining two bits of body together, perhaps knee to knee, unjoining them to make a line between the knees, replacing the line with your lower leg or with your arm, inverting the line, or elongating it, or surrounding it, or contracting it, basically drawing geometrically in space in an organised and unexpected way to make beautiful, virtuosic movement.

I wanted to share the hidden narrative that dancers may have behind their moves. Our narrative was lighthearted, two dancers waking up and coming to rehearsal, in their own way: 'Putting on my shirt, where are my shoes, wash my face, lock my front door, jump on the first bus, miss the second, push through the crowds, breathe fresh air...' Form it, put it altogether, phrase it and you have two dazzling phrases of apparently plotless dance and yet they intrigue.

We obviously succeeded in giving insight in some measure for the next thing I knew the BBC had heard of the event and were contemplating making an informative programme. You never know who is watching what you do or reading what you write. Surprising outcomes sometimes come your way. The documentary for BBC4, 'Dance Rebels', directed by Bernadette O'Brien was one such surprise for before I knew what was what I was in front of her camera.

The hazard is 'they' ask the questions and film for a morning, then pick what 'they' want for the overarching story line, perhaps one phrase, perhaps a laugh, perhaps more, meanwhile you sign away your reputation. Bernadette's ruthless editing told the story of one twentieth century dance rebel after another, choreographers who rejected the old, introduced something new, starting by leaving the nineteenth century values of classical ballet and embracing the modernity that dominated the twentieth century and on to the digital twenty-first.

Apparently Bernadette was interested in what I could convey, could illustrate. Having been in the dance business for so many years, known so many choreographers, I was happy to ad lib quite informally and function in a studio to camera, where a less experienced person might need a text or suffer camera freeze. I was amused when, in the last weeks of editing, BBC4 were short of a telling ending. Bernadette's boss emailed, 'Get back that old biddy who laughs'. Me. So I ended up having the last word of the ninety-minute documentary.

'Dance Rebels' was aired in December 2015. It served one clear purpose for me. It seemed that for the first time, literally, my wider family and non-dance friends who had never understood what I got up to, finally got the message, so thank you Bernadette O'Brien.

In Memoriam 2014

Supported by **Trinity Laban Conservatoire of Music and Dance** and **Dorothy Witney Elmhirst Trust**.

Chapter 0:
Introduction

Chapter 1:
Entrance

Chapter 2:
Celebration of difference

Chapter 3:
Confrontation of d

In Memoriam 2014 on the Internet

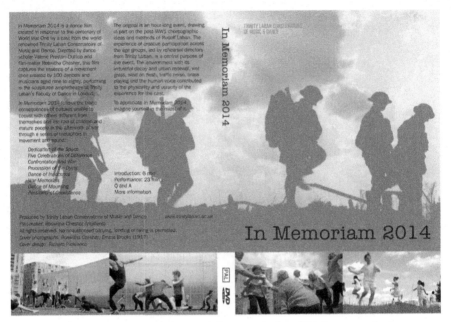

The DVD cover for *In Memoriam 2014* (Design Richard Pickvance, photos Roswitha Chesher, Ernest Brooks)

Speaking informally to camera

CHAPTER 25

2016

Monte Verita

Staggering in at 1.00 am after a journey confounded by fog, ice and delay I wondered why I still accept invitations to fly round the globe to share my knowledge with the younger generation. But I do and this trip was to Switzerland.

Monte Verita in the Ticino rises from the shores of Lake Maggiore surrounded by blue mountains and silence. There, in 1912, contemporary dance was born, as Rudolf Laban began his quest to emancipate dance from its heritage of music visualisation and ballet's fixed lexicon of steps and conventions. The year 1912 proved to be a remarkable one in which significant artists in music, art and dance faced the new century with change as their key motivation.

That year *The Rite of Spring* erupted from the score of Igor Stravinsky. If ever I am asked for my Desert Island Discs Stravinsky would feature for we students danced our version of the *Rite*, or bits of it, causing consternation to the visiting Inspector of Education. Vaslav Nijinsky had astounded the Parisian elite with ugly, angular, heavy clumping dance. *Rite* caused a furore. Less riotous but nevertheless ugly, ours caused sharp intakes of breath by the audience in Manchester. One fellow student who did have *The Rite* in her Desert Island Discs was Joan Plowright, who thumped the floor with the rest of us before moving on to her illustrious career as an actress and marrying Laurence Olivier.

Abstract paintings adorn the walls of my flat, a large print of Hans Hoffman's *Golden Wall* inspiring me daily. We have to thank Wassily Kandinsky who introduced abstraction, publishing *Concerning the Spiritual in Art* in 1912, where form and colour for the first time were presented as meaningful in their own right. Meaning became a fascinating conundrum and still is, with the straightforward still life, portrait and landscape abandoned and the open-ended signification of blue and red, angle and curve, ordered and chaotic form, taking their place. My visitors ponder my walls, some appreciative some confounded. I do not have a lamb in formaldehyde nor do I invite them to regard my untidy bedroom as an art object, but next year?

In 1912 in Dresden Jaques-Dalcroze directed a performance using his style of music-derived dance, *Eurythmics*. Causing a considerable stir in the international audience he proposed his method as suitable for a new dance form for the twentieth century. I recall attending a eurythmics summer school aged sixteen that my dear mother thought might be a suitable preparation for my impending studentship at the new Laban school. How wrong she was, for my teenage soul was about to experience the sort of seismic shock offered on Monte Verita in 1912, as Laban rejected Dalcroze's method.

On the Mountain of Truth this year I was asked to introduce the DVD *Living Architecture* that I directed with Anna Carlisle in 2008. *Living Architecture* illustrates how Laban embodied spiritual values in dance sequences by paying attention to the harmony contained in the symmetries and proportions of abstract movement. Lifting your arm above your head can be just that or it can be a reaching towards the cosmos. Bending down can be just that or it can be touching base with mother earth. And so on. The choice is, stay in the material world or inhabit the infinite and the latter is where *Living Architecture* is.

I first learned these spatial movements in my teenage years and loved them. They could transform the reality of being cold, in a grubby studio, in foggy Manchester, into the world I first entered with Miss Moore aged four, and still enter in 2016 in Monte Verita, and in Blackheath when I dance in my sitting room.

It was 1949 when I began to understand what caused this transformational magic. Laban's researches had discovered the spatial forms he named the 7-rings, alternating movements that shoot out into space with movements that encircle you. The experience of these forms gives you such a satisfactory sense of the balance of opposites, up with down, open with closed, angle with curve, sharp with smooth, that they send shivers down my spine.

'Val, you write them', Laban had said so as part of my apprenticeship I notated the 7-rings and made them into a card that he sent as a thank you for the good wishes he received from all over the world for his 70th birthday. So, yes, I value passing on this knowledge to young people. They are interested because it touches something in their gut. I would say it touches their soul, you might put it another way.

On a piece of open ground on Monte Verita now stands a man-sized icosahedron, the twenty-faced geometric 3D form in and around which the 7-rings and their fellow 3-, 5- and 12-rings circulate. And have their being. My pleasure is that Nunzia Tirelli persuaded the hotel manager and other people in positions of power in the canton Ticino that a permanent memorial to Laban's incredible innovations and insights at Monte Verita might be put. And put it was. My pleasure primarily is that I have been able to pass on to people, including Nunzia, some of the values that have nourished my life. That sounds mundane, doesn't every mother do that, every teacher do that, every soul with a passion?

Perhaps the fact that John's and my wedding cake was adorned with an icosahedron in place of traditional decorative icing was a way of stating that my values were not an option. For some wedding guests the cake was bizarre, a bit of a joke, but for a few an insight into a quest that has continued into my eighties.

Plato it was who identified the five perfect solids of which the icosahedron is one. In the Monte Verita lecture theatre I listened to a presentation for the local intellectuals on Plato, in Italian, a bit of a strain, but recovered, participating in a calm choreutic meditation event where young and old, knowledgeable or a beginner, can share the perfection of spatially harmonic movement.

And now, onwards, my favourite word, onwards to the next endeavour whatever that will be.

On Monte Verita with the new icosahedron and the next generation of dance pioneers, from l. Rosemary Brandt (GB), Paola Napolitano, Nunzia Tirelli (Switzerland), Sylvie Robaldo (France), Debora di Cento (Italy), Evelyn Dörr (Germany), Alison Curtis-Jones (GB) (Ph. Paolo Tosi)

Celebrating my 85th birthday with the family, Venetia's shot of Polly, me, Emma and Roger in the grounds of the Old Naval College, Greenwich

My grandchildren Polly and Jack, facing forward and getting on with life

Concentrating on the talk on Plato in Monte Verita's lecture theatre (Ph. Paolo Tosi)

Participating in a choreutic meditation at Monte Verita (Ph. Paolo Tosi)

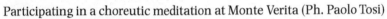

Index

References to illustrations are given in italics.

Lightning Source UK Ltd.
Milton Keynes UK
UKOW05n2144120617
303205UK00009B/60/P

9 781906 830809